SLOW COOKING
for TWO

SLOW COOKING
for TWO
Basics
Techniques
Recipes

Cynthia Graubart

Photographs by Christopher Hornaday

GIBBS SMITH
TO ENRICH AND INSPIRE HUMANKIND

First Edition
17 16 15 14 13   5 4 3 2 1

Text © 2013 by Cynthia Graubart
Photographs © 2013 by Christopher Hornaday

Published by
Gibbs Smith
P.O. Box 667
Layton, Utah 84041

1.800.835.4993 orders
www.gibbs-smith.com

Design by Debra McQuiston
Page production by Renee Bond
Printed and bound in Hong Kong
Gibbs Smith books are printed on paper produced
from sustainable PEFC-certified forest/controlled
wood source. Learn more at www.pefc.org.

Library of Congress Cataloging-in-Publication Data

Graubart, Cynthia Stevens.
  Slow cooking for two : basics techniques recipes
/ Cynthia Graubart ; photographs by Christopher
Hornaday. — First edition.
      pages cm
  Includes index.
  ISBN 978-1-4236-3383-9
  1. Electric cooking, Slow. 2. Cooking for two. I. Title.
  TX827.G75 2013
  641.5'884—dc23
                          2013005926

ACKNOWLEDGMENTS

My husband, Cliff Graubart, is a prince. Without him we would not have had meals to eat while I was writing, or a clean kitchen while I was testing. To Nathalie Dupree, I owe a debt of gratitude for her generosity, and for the idea of Double Dinners. Catherine Fliegel, my first co-author and friend, is a wonderful proofreader. Photographer Christopher Hornaday, food stylist Nan McCulloch, and assistant Jill Heiser made my maiden voyage in food photography an absolute pleasure. My editor Madge Baird suggested this book and I couldn't have been more delighted to work with her again. The mistakes here are all my own. And thank you to Cuisinart, Hamilton Beach, and Rival, for the slow cookers used in testing.

CONTENTS

INTRODUCTION

It was 1974 when the avocado-green Rival brand Crock-Pot entered my life and became a boon to our family. My mother was working full time and attending nursing school part time, and the mere thought of dinner preparing itself was enormously liberating.

Rooting around the dark corners of the kitchen cabinets several years later as I headed off to college, I pilfered the Crock-Pot. It turned out not to be so handy: the meals served far too many portions and I hated having leftovers for days at a time. The crock itself was attached to the base, so washing the inside without getting the appliance wet was a nuisance.

Years later, raising my own family caused me to revisit the concept. I replaced the green beast with a new 6-quart model with modern features, like multiple heat settings and an auto-switch-to-warm setting. I even included a chapter on slow cooking in my first book, *The One-Armed Cook,* co-authored with Catherine Fliegel, and touted it as a much more useful choice for a baby shower registry gift than a baby wipes warmer!

So steadfast was my devotion that I continued to slow cook even as my children left the nest, but I found myself right back in that "leftovers for days" quandary. Life was just as hectic as ever, and I needed those days when I could leave something to cook unattended.

Enter the newest addition to my kitchen, the 3½-quart slow cooker! I can now prepare reasonable-quantity slow-cooked meals while I go about my busy day.

This book is intended for newlyweds, empty nesters, small apartments, and unusual spaces where a slow cooker might be the only appliance available for cooking (vacation cabin, boat, RV). The recipes do not call for browning or other additional preparation steps requiring another appliance such and a stove, oven or microwave. Each recipe is designed for 2, with a little leftover for lunch or perhaps a second light meal or a third drop-in diner. All of the ingredients can be found in your local grocery store, without an extra trip to a specialty store. And although this is not a Southern slow cooker book, my Southern cooking bias is surely evident.

Slow cooking is an ideal cooking method to tenderize tough cuts of meat. It's also a boon to the busy cook who could benefit from a recipe that cooks unattended. A slow cooker uses about the same amount of electricity as a 75-watt bulb.

ABOUT SLOW COOKERS
SELECTING A SLOW COOKER

Slow cookers are available in many sizes, from just 1-quart all the way up to 7-quart. For a typical family, a 5- to 7-quart size is ideal, but still too large for cooking for 2. I found the best size for me is the 3½-quart slow cooker. There are a few choices in that size range; I like one with these handy features:

- High, Low, Warm, and Off settings
- Programmable Timer
- Auto switch to Warm at the end of cooking time
- Power indicator light
- See-through lid
- Removable crock
- Oval shape (more accommodating to irregular-shaped foods)

All the recipes in this book were tested in the Cuisinart brand 3½-quart slow cooker, which has all the above features.

SLOW COOKER SAFETY

Read the manufacturer's guide that came with your slow cooker. It contains information unique to your slow cooker.

Never use an extension cord to plug in your slow cooker. The cord is purposefully short to prevent accidental turning over of the appliance.

The outside of a slow cooker gets hot, so keep it away from children and pets, low-hanging cabinets, and walls.

Do not wash a slow cooker insert until it has cooled *or the pot might crack.*

WHAT'S DIFFERENT ABOUT THIS BOOK?

Double Dinners—Most cuts of beef and chicken parts are sold in packages designed to serve 4 or more people. Since I dislike having a large quantity of leftovers, I've designed Double Dinners. These recipes call for using slow cooker liners as separate cooking bags to cook two different recipes in the same slow cooker at the same time, using the total package amount of meat. For example, the smallest chuck roast available in my local grocery store is 2–2½ pounds. By cutting the roast into two equal portions and following two separate recipes, I have two completely different dinners from the same roast, cooked at the same time in the same slow cooker—one for dinner tonight and one for a future meal that's not a leftover! (see page 67).

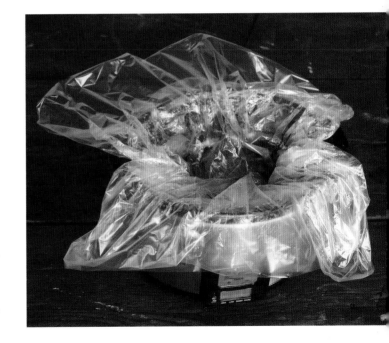

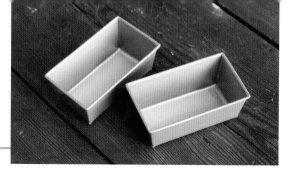

Mini Loaf Pan

A RECIPE FOR SUCCESS
ADDITIONAL EQUIPMENT

These items can be found in a well-stocked suburban grocery store, obtained at your local cookware shop, or easily ordered online:

- Immersion Blender—I'm not a gadget geek and keep very few specialty gadgets in my kitchen. I thought an immersion blender fell into that category until I started using one! Pureeing a soup is now a breeze without having to transfer hot solids into a blender or food processor. Add one to your kitchen if you can; I doubt you'll regret it.
- Mini loaf pan—A 5½ x 3-inch pan is perfect for the banana-nut bread.
- 5-inch-diameter cake pan—My pan is nonstick, but I still line it with wax paper to create the chocolate and lemon cakes.
- 4-cup glass dish—Glass storage dishes, also made for reheating, are great for the perfect lemon curd.
- 2 (½-cup) ramekins—Look for either glass custard cups or porcelain ramekins to make the chocolate mousse or lemon cream.

5-inch Diameter Cake Pan

4 Cup Glass Dishes

½-Cup Ramekins

Slow Cooker Liners

- Slow cooker liners—Popular for easy cleanup, these are the basis for my Double Dinners (page 67).
- Aluminum foil—Handy for the foil sling to help remove meatloaves from the slow cooker.
- Instant-read thermometer—I wouldn't be without one. This is an essential tool to be sure your meat and poultry reach a safe temperature.

To Make a Foil Sling

Cut two 6-inch wide strips of aluminum foil. Take a strip and fold it over lengthwise into thirds, creating a long 2-inch-wide strip. Repeat with second strip. Place the strips into the slow cooker, crossing each other. The ends will help form a sling to remove the contents of the slow cooker.

Foil Sling

To Make a Foil Ring

Cut a 1- to 2-inch strip of aluminum foil. Crumple the strip lengthwise and form into a circle. Place at the bottom of the slow cooker to keep the bottom of a pan or dish from coming into direct contact with the bottom of the slow cooker. Optionally, a metal object such as a canning jar ring or a cookie cutter can be used.

Options for Raising Dishes off of Slow Cooker Bottom

IMPORTANT RECIPE TIPS

A common complaint about slow cooker recipes is that they all taste the same or look the same. While it's true that what a slow cooker does best is the long, slow braise, which usually means a beef roast is involved, there are ingredients to further jazz up your recipes, all added at the end of cooking. Stir in any of the following:

- Additional chopped fresh herbs
- Grated lemon or lime rind
- A little extra garlic
- A dash of soy sauce, sriracha, pesto, or other ready-made sauce
- A dollop of tomato paste
- A bit of chopped cooked bacon
- A little extra grated cheese, usually Parmesan
- Always season to taste at the end of cooking with more salt and pepper

Don't lift the lid during cooking, unless directed by the recipe, or you'll need to add 20 minutes to the cooking time.

Dense root vegetables, like potatoes, cook more slowly than meat in the slow cooker, so put in the cooker first, on the bottom and closest to the heat.

Don't fill slow cookers to the top. They cook most efficiently when they are half to three-quarters full.

COOKING TIMES

Different slow cookers vary in their temperature range. Most slow cookers reach a temperature of 300 degrees on High, and 200 degrees on Low. Some cook fast (at a higher temperature) and some cook slow (at a lower temperature). You'll have to adjust cooking times to the quirks of your slow cooker. This can be a little frustrating at first, so allow some flexibility in the finishing time of a recipe the first time you make it—it might be ready a little earlier—or a little later—than expected. Once you know how your slow cooker operates, you'll be able to adjust the recipe cooking times accordingly.

Read the recipe all the way through before cooking, and assemble all ingredients.

If you are transporting your dish to serve at a different location, plan to use a liner so you can tie the liner closed before transporting the meal in the slow cooker, thus precluding a nasty spill.

FAVORITE NON-SLOW COOKER RECIPES

Here's a handy chart for converting your non-slow cooker recipes. A recipe that is normally braised on the stove or in the oven is a good candidate for the slow cooker.

CONVENTIONAL RECIPE TIME	SLOW COOKER TIME ON LOW
15 minutes	1½ to 2 hours
20 minutes	2 to 3 hours
30 minutes	3 to 4 hours
45 minutes	5 to 6 hours
60 minutes	6 to 8 hours
90 minutes	8 to 9 hours
2 hours	9 to 10 hours

FREQUENTLY ASKED QUESTIONS

Do I have to check on the slow cooker while it's cooking?

The first time you use your slow cooker, plan to be home. That way you'll be there to notice any quirks of your appliance. After that, you can leave the slow cooker to do the work alone.

Do I have to stir?

Luckily, stirring is not necessary during cooking, unless specifically indicated in the recipe. In fact, lifting the lid to stir when it's not indicated will increase the cooking time by 20 minutes.

Does the slow cooker stop automatically?

Only if you have a programmable machine, which I highly recommend. Otherwise, set a timer so you can be ready to turn your slow cooker to Warm or Off.

What if I overcook the recipe?

A slow cooker is very forgiving. Usually the cooking times are for a range of time, so not to worry. All the recipes in this book will specify if there is a danger of overcooking.

How long can a recipe sit in the slow cooker?

The programmable slow cookers are set to turn automatically to the Warm setting after cooking. They then switch to Off after 2 hours. As a general rule, food should not sit for more than 2 hours after cooking, or there is an increased risk of bacteria growing.

Can I convert my own recipes to the slow cooker?

Yes, but primarily they should be recipes based on long, slow cooking on the stove or in the oven, with liquid to help create steam. See the rough conversion chart on page 15.

Can I bake in my slow cooker?
Yes! Be sure to check out the cake and bread recipes in this book. Experiment to come up with new recipes.

Can I double these recipes?
Absolutely, but don't completely double the liquid used in a recipe; add only about 50% more liquid. Increase the cooking time about an hour, checking to be sure the food is cooked to the normal temperature and consistency, and increasing the time if necessary.

Since some of these recipes can be made faster in the oven or on the stove. Why should I bother with the slow cooker?
Because a slow cooker is so forgiving, there's a lot less pressure to be right there waiting to remove a dish before it gets overcooked, or to stand at the stove stirring constantly. The granola (see page 130), for instance, can easily burn in a conventional oven but would require considerable overcooking to burn in a slow cooker.

THE SLOW COOKER PANTRY

I'm a firm believer in a well-stocked pantry. It's especially handy when life gets in the way of my plans. The recipes in this book are based on pantry staples, ensuring you'll have the ingredients on hand.

REFRIGERATOR

- **Dairy**—butter, milk, half-and-half or heavy cream, sour cream or crème fraîche, a variety of cheeses (blocks to freshly grate, or already grated or shredded). Parmigiano-Reggiano is the king of all Parmesan cheese, and its extraordinary taste is well worth the extra expense.
- **Vegetables**—a variety of fresh herbs (basil, chives, cilantro, oregano, parsley, rosemary, tarragon, thyme), carrots, celery, bell peppers, hot peppers, eggplant, ginger, kale, spinach, leeks, lemons, limes, mushrooms, and zucchini

- **Condiments**—ketchup, Worcestershire sauce, soy sauce, Dijon mustard, hoisin sauce, favorite hot sauce, salsa, horseradish
- Fully-cooked bacon

DRY PANTRY

- Garlic, shallots, and onion
- Russet, red, new, and sweet potatoes
- Canned tomatoes in a variety of preparations—whole, crushed, diced, tomato sauce
- Marinated artichoke hearts
- Dried fruits and tomatoes
- Flour (all-purpose and self-rising), cornstarch, and/or quick-cooking tapioca for thickening sauces
- Brown and white sugars, honey
- Breadcrumbs
- Broths—chicken, beef, and vegetable
- Red and white wine, dry sherry, port
- Vinegars—white, red wine, balsamic
- Oils—olive oil, other cooking oil
- Chipotle chile in adobo, canned green chilis

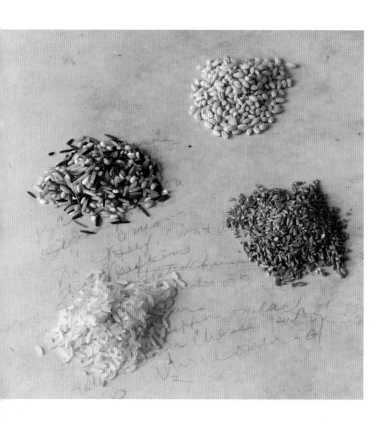

- Uncooked converted rice, wild rice, Arborio rice, pearl barley, bulgur wheat
- Dried lentils

- Canned black beans, cannellini beans, kidney beans
- Peanut butter
- Nuts—almonds, pecans, walnuts
- Capers, olives
- Jams and jellies
- Spices—allspice, bay leaf, chili powder, Chinese five-spice powder, ground cinnamon, ground cloves, ground coriander, ground cumin, Italian seasoning, ground nutmeg, ground sage, red pepper flakes

FREEZER

- Vegetables—corn, chopped onion, herbs
- Meats—flank steak, chuck roast, short ribs, pork tenderloin, beef and lamb stew meat, kielbasa
- Poultry—boneless skinless chicken breasts, skinless chicken thighs, boneless skinless chicken thighs, Cornish hen, turkey legs, turkey tenderloins, ground chicken and turkey
- Orange juice concentrate

SOUPS

POTATO AND LEEK SOUP

SERVES 2

Thick and hearty potato soup is a comfort to the soul. Popular in French cuisine, this classic potato and leek combination has the satisfaction of a peasant dish and a taste fit for a king.

Thank you, Julia Child, for the inspiration.

1 tablespoon butter, room temperature
1 medium leek, white part and some light
   green, chopped
1 large baking potato, peeled and diced
1 cup chicken broth
1/3 cup half-and-half
Salt
Freshly ground black pepper
Sour cream or crème fraîche, optional
Chopped fresh or freeze-dried chives or
   parsley, optional

1. Coat the inside of a 3^1/$_2$-quart slow cooker with cooking spray, if desired.

2. Turn the slow cooker on High and add the butter. When the butter has melted, add the leek and stir to coat in the butter. Add the potato and broth. Stir well to mix. Turn the slow cooker to the Low heat setting.

3. Cover and cook on Low for 6 hours. Remove lid and puree soup using an immersion blender (or remove the solids with a slotted spoon to a blender or food processor and puree until smooth; then return puree to slow cooker).

4. Whisk in the half-and-half. Allow the soup to sit uncovered 10 to 15 minutes while it heats. Whisk again and season to taste with salt and pepper.

5. When ready to serve, top individual bowls with a portion of sour cream or crème fraîche, if desired, and sprinkle with optional chopped chives or parsley.

PREPARING THE LEEK

Trim off the root end, keeping the leaves attached. Cut off tops so the leek is 6 to 7 inches long. Starting 1/2 inch from the root end and keeping leaves attached, slit leek lengthwise in half and then in quarters. Wash under cold running water, spreading the leaves apart to rinse off all dirt. Slice leeks crosswise into 1/2-inch pieces for the soup.

FIRE-ROASTED TOMATO SOUP
SERVES 2

Ingredients that come with an extra layer of flavor already built in, as with these fire-roasted diced tomatoes, can jump-start a recipe. This creamy soup might call out for a grilled cheese sandwich on the side.

¼ cup chopped onion
2 cloves garlic, minced, or 1 teaspoon
    bottled minced garlic
1 (14½-ounce) can fire-roasted diced
    tomatoes, drained
¼ cup chicken broth or red wine
2 tablespoons olive oil
2 tablespoons chopped fresh basil, or
    2 teaspoons dried basil
Pinch of red pepper flakes, optional
¼ cup ricotta cheese
½ cup half-and-half
Salt
Freshly ground black pepper
Grated or shredded Parmesan cheese,
    optional

1. Coat the inside of a 3½-quart slow cooker with cooking spray, if desired.

2. Add the onion, garlic, tomatoes, broth or wine, olive oil, basil, and optional red pepper flakes. Stir well to mix.

3. Cover and cook on Low for 4 hours.

4. Remove the lid and puree the soup using an immersion blender (or remove the solids with a slotted spoon to a blender or food processor and puree until smooth; then return puree to slow cooker).

5. Whisk in the ricotta cheese and half-and-half. Allow soup to sit uncovered 15 to 20 minutes while the soup reheats. Whisk again, and season to taste with salt and pepper.

6. When ready to serve, top individual bowls with a portion of the Parmesan cheese, if desired.

LENTIL, TOMATO, AND RICE SOUP

SERVES 2

Adapted from a recipe by Katie Workman, author of *The Mom 100 Cookbook*, this soup is made from pantry staples, so you're likely to have the ingredients on hand. Vegetarian broth may be substituted for the chicken broth, and water or additional broth may be substituted for the wine. Check the lentils for any small pebbles and remove before adding to the slow cooker. Stir once during cooking, if desired.

$\frac{1}{4}$ cup chopped onion

1 medium carrot, chopped

$\frac{1}{4}$ cup uncooked converted rice

1 sprig fresh thyme, or $\frac{1}{4}$ teaspoon dried thyme

Splash of wine, dry white or red

$\frac{1}{2}$ clove garlic, minced, or $\frac{1}{4}$ teaspoon bottled minced garlic

1 (14$\frac{1}{2}$-ounce) can crushed tomatoes

1$\frac{1}{2}$ cups chicken broth

$\frac{1}{4}$ cup dried lentils, picked over

Salt

Freshly ground black pepper

Crumbled feta cheese, optional

1. Coat the inside of a 3$\frac{1}{2}$-quart slow cooker with cooking spray, if desired.

2. Add the onion, carrot, rice, thyme, wine, garlic, tomatoes, broth, and lentils. Stir well to mix.

3. Cover and cook on Low for 7 hours.

4. When ready to serve, remove thyme sprig, and season to taste with salt and pepper. Top individual bowls with a portion of the feta cheese, if desired.

SMOKY CHIPOTLE BUTTERNUT SQUASH SOUP

SERVES 2

The influence of the Latino culture in American cuisine is now broad and deep. Achieving a deep, smoky, spicy flavor in the slow cooker can be a challenge, but Sandra Gutierrez, author of *The New Southern Latino Table,* a fine cook and cooking teacher, inspired me to adapt her butternut squash soup recipe. We season mildly in our house, so bump up the chipotle chile to your liking.

1 (12-ounce) package frozen butternut squash, thawed
1/4 cup chopped onion
1 clove garlic, minced, or 1/2 teaspoon bottled minced garlic
1/2 teaspoon ground sage
1/2 teaspoon chipotle chile in adobo, or more to taste
1 1/2 cups chicken broth
1/2 cup half-and-half
Salt
Freshly ground black pepper
1 or 2 slices pre-cooked bacon, finely chopped

1. Coat the inside of a 3 1/2-quart slow cooker with cooking spray, if desired.

2. Add the squash, onion, garlic, sage, chili, and chicken broth. Stir well to mix.

3. Cover and cook on Low for 4 hours.

4. Remove lid and puree soup using an immersion blender (or remove to a blender or food processor and puree until smooth; then return puree to slow cooker).

5. Whisk in the half-and-half. Allow soup to sit uncovered 15 to 20 minutes while it heats. Whisk again, and season to taste with salt and pepper.

6. When ready to serve, top individual bowls of soup with bacon.

CHIPOTLE CHILES IN ADOBO

Available in small cans, these chiles really bring on the heat. Our family seasons on the mild side, so we have a gracious plenty left over. Separate the remaining chiles from the can onto a sheet of wax paper, cutting each in half if desired. Freeze until solid, then remove to a resealable plastic bag or freezer container. Similar in concept to freezing leftover tomato paste in tablespoons, this eliminates waste and keeps a lesser used ingredient on hand for future use.

BLACK BEAN SOUP

SERVES 2

Thick and hearty, beefy enough for meat lovers but vegetarian friendly, this black bean soup uses the convenience of canned beans. The sour cream and salsa are wonderful but still optional.

1/4 cup chopped onion

1 rib celery, chopped

1 small carrot, chopped or thinly sliced

1 clove garlic, minced, or 1/2 teaspoon bottled minced garlic

1 teaspoon chopped fresh basil, or 1/2 teaspoon dried basil

1 teaspoon chopped fresh oregano, or 1/2 teaspoon dried oregano

1/4 teaspoon ground cumin

1/4 teaspoon chili powder

1 (15-ounce) can black beans, rinsed and drained

1 1/2 cups chicken broth

1 (8-ounce) can tomato sauce

1/4 cup uncooked converted rice

Salt

Freshly ground black pepper

Sour cream, optional

Salsa, optional

1. Coat the inside of a 3 1/2-quart slow cooker with cooking spray, if desired.

2. Add the onion, celery, carrot, garlic, herbs, cumin, chili powder, beans, broth, tomato sauce, and rice. Stir well to mix.

3. Cover and cook on Low for 6 hours.

4. When ready to serve, season to taste with salt and pepper. Top individual bowls with a portion of the sour cream and/or salsa, if desired.

KALE AND KIELBASA SOUP

SERVES 2+

Turkey kielbasa sausage is readily available in the refrigerated cured/cooked meats section of your grocery store. High in protein and relatively low in fat, it is a hearty addition to this soup, creating a more stew-like dish. The leftovers are worthwhile to have around. They freeze, if necessary, in an airtight container for up to three months.

1 (15-ounce) can cannellini beans, rinsed and drained

¼ cup chopped onion

1 clove garlic, minced, or ½ teaspoon bottled minced garlic

1 sprig fresh rosemary, or ¼ teaspoon dried rosemary

1 cup chicken broth

½ cup chopped fresh tomatoes, or canned diced tomatoes

7 ounces turkey kielbasa, cut into ½-inch slices

1–2 cups chopped fresh kale

Salt

Freshly ground black pepper

Grated or shredded Parmesan cheese, optional

1. Coat the inside of a 3½-quart slow cooker with cooking spray, if desired.

2. Add the beans, onion, garlic, rosemary, broth, tomatoes, kielbasa, and kale. Stir well to mix.

3. Cover and cook on Low for 7 hours.

4. When ready to serve, remove rosemary sprig, and season to taste with salt and pepper. Top individual bowls of soup with Parmesan cheese, if desired.

HAMBURGER SOUP

SERVES 2

This one-pot meal has been a family favorite for years—even when the children were very young. Now I've adapted it for just my husband and me and let the slow cooker do all the work. Fresh parsley or another favorite fresh herb brightens the flavor of the finished soup.

1/4 cup chopped onion
1/2 pound lean ground beef
1 rib celery, chopped
1 small carrot, chopped or thinly sliced
1 medium baking potato, peeled, and diced
1 (14-ounce) can beef broth
1 (14 1/2-ounce) can whole tomatoes
1 bay leaf
1 sprig fresh thyme, or 1/4 teaspoon dried thyme
Salt
Freshly ground black pepper
Chopped fresh or freeze-dried parsley, optional

1. Coat the inside of a 3 1/2-quart slow cooker with cooking spray, if desired.

2. Add the onion and ground beef. Using a metal spoon or spatula, break the ground beef into small pieces. Add celery, carrot, potato, broth, tomatoes, bay leaf, and thyme. Stir well to mix.

3. Cover and cook on Low for 5 hours.

4. When ready to serve, remove thyme sprig, and season to taste with salt and pepper. Top individual bowls with parsley, if desired.

POULTRY

PEANUT CHICKEN

SERVES 2

Chicken breasts turn stringy if cooked too long in a slow cooker. Chicken is fully cooked when the internal temperature of the thickest part of the chicken reaches 165 degrees on an instant-read thermometer. These breasts are tender and moist and fully cooked after just 3$\frac{1}{2}$ hours on the Low heat setting. Coat a measuring cup with cooking spray and the peanut butter will slide right out.

2 boneless, skinless chicken breasts
Salt
Freshly ground black pepper
1 red bell pepper, cored, seeded, and chopped
$\frac{1}{4}$ cup chopped onion
$\frac{1}{3}$ cup peanut butter
1 teaspoon ground cumin
1 teaspoon ground coriander
Juice of 1 lime, or 2 tablespoon bottled lime juice
$\frac{1}{3}$ cup soy sauce
$\frac{1}{4}$ cup white wine
$\frac{1}{4}$ cup chopped fresh cilantro, optional
$\frac{1}{4}$ cup chopped peanuts, optional

1. Coat the inside of a 3$\frac{1}{2}$-quart slow cooker with cooking spray, if desired.

2. Sprinkle the chicken breasts liberally with salt and pepper. Transfer to slow cooker.

3. Add the bell pepper and onion to slow cooker.

4. Stir together remaining ingredients, except optional ingredients, in a small bowl. Pour over chicken in slow cooker.

5. Cover and cook on Low for 3$\frac{1}{2}$ hours.

6. Taste, and season again with salt and pepper. Serve chicken with cooking liquid, topped with cilantro and peanuts, if desired.

LEMON CHICKEN

SERVES 2

My friend and cookbook author Catherine Fliegel would make her famous Lemon Chicken when we would get together with our kids for a family dinner. Her recipe was breaded and sautéed, and delicious. When I make this recipe, the lemon shines through and makes me think of her and those wonderful evenings together.

2 boneless, skinless chicken breasts
Salt
Freshly ground black pepper
2 teaspoons fresh lemon juice
1 garlic clove, minced, or $1/2$ teaspoon
    bottled minced garlic
1 tablespoon capers, drained
$1/4$ cup chicken broth
$1/4$ cup white wine

1. Coat the inside of a $3^1/2$-quart slow cooker with cooking spray, if desired.

2. Sprinkle chicken breasts liberally with salt and pepper. Transfer to slow cooker.

3. Stir together remaining ingredients in a small bowl and pour over chicken in slow cooker.

4. Cover and cook on Low for $3^1/2$ hours.

5. Taste, and season again with salt and pepper. Serve chicken with cooking liquid.

6. If a thicker sauce is desired, add 1 tablespoon cornstarch to a small bowl and stir in $1/4$ cup liquid from slow cooker until cornstarch is fully dissolved and incorporated. Remove chicken to a serving platter and cover loosely with foil. Stir the cornstarch mixture into the cooking liquid. Turn the heat setting to High and leave the cover off. The liquid will thicken slightly into a sauce after about 15 minutes. Serve sauce over chicken.

OPTIONAL:
Stir 1 (5-ounce) bag baby spinach into the hot finished sauce until wilted, and serve over chicken.

CHICKEN IN CILANTRO RED PEPPER SAUCE

SERVES 2

The red bell pepper mellows in the slow cooker and once pureed becomes a piquant sauce for the chicken. If you are not a fan, omit the cilantro.

2 boneless, skinless chicken breasts
Salt
Freshly ground black pepper
1/4 cup chopped onion
1 red bell pepper, cored, seeded, and sliced
1 clove garlic, minced, or 1/2 teaspoon bottled minced garlic
1 (14 1/2-ounce) can diced tomatoes
1 tablespoon chopped fresh cilantro, divided, optional
1/2 cup chicken broth

1. Coat the inside of a 3 1/2-quart slow cooker with cooking spray, if desired.

2. Sprinkle chicken breasts liberally with salt and pepper. Transfer to slow cooker.

3. Stir the onion, bell pepper, garlic, tomatoes, 1/2 tablespoon of the optional cilantro, and chicken stock together in a medium bowl. Mix well and pour over chicken in slow cooker.

4. Cover and cook on Low for 3 1/2 hours.

5. Remove chicken to a serving platter and cover loosely with foil to keep warm. Use an immersion blender to puree remaining liquid and vegetables. Taste, and season again with salt and pepper. Serve over chicken. Sprinkle with remaining cilantro, if desired.

CHICKEN BOG

SERVES 2

My friend, cookbook author Rebecca Lang, calls this the official chicken soup of the South. The original recipe appears in her book *Around My Southern Table* and is the inspiration here, but using only chicken breasts rather than a whole chicken.

2 boneless, skinless chicken breasts
Salt
Freshly ground black pepper
1 rib celery, chopped
1/4 cup chopped onion
1 medium carrot, chopped or thinly sliced
1 clove garlic, minced, or 1/2 teaspoon
   bottled minced garlic
1 bay leaf
1/2 cup uncooked converted white rice
4 cups chicken broth
1 green onion, white and some green part,
   thinly sliced, divided
Finely chopped fresh or freeze-dried
   parsley, optional

1. Coat the inside of a 3 1/2-quart slow cooker with cooking spray, if desired.

2. Sprinkle chicken breasts liberally with salt and pepper. Transfer to slow cooker.

3. Add the celery, onion, carrot, garlic, bay leaf, and rice. Pour in chicken broth.

4. Cover and cook on Low for 3 1/2 hours.

5. Remove and discard bay leaf. Remove chicken to a cutting board, cut into chunks, and return to slow cooker, stirring the chicken into the rice. Stir half the green onion into the bog.

6. Taste, and season again with salt and pepper. Top individual bowls of bog with the remaining green onion and chopped parsley, if using, before serving.

CHICKEN THIGHS IN DIJON ARTICHOKE SAUCE

SERVES 2

Chicken skin doesn't brown or crisp in the slow cooker, but left on the bone, chicken thighs are flavorful, tender, and moist. Tarragon is one of my favorite herbs and it marries well with Dijon mustard. Drain the artichokes well before chopping and adding to the slow cooker.

4 bone-in, skinless chicken thighs

$1/4$ cup Dijon mustard

1 clove garlic, minced, or $1/2$ teaspoon bottled minced garlic

$1/2$ tablespoon chopped fresh tarragon, or $1/2$ teaspoon dried tarragon

$1/4$ cup chopped onion

1 cup sliced fresh mushrooms

1 (6-ounce) jar marinated artichoke hearts, drained and chopped

Salt

Freshly ground black pepper

$1/4$ cup white wine

1. Coat the inside of a $3^1/2$-quart slow cooker with cooking spray, if desired.

2. Stir together the mustard, garlic, and tarragon in a large bowl. Add the chicken thighs and stir well to coat. Add the onion, mushrooms, and artichokes. Season to taste with salt and pepper. Pour in wine and add all to the slow cooker.

4. Cover and cook on High for 4 hours.

5. Taste, and season again with salt and pepper. Serve chicken with sauce.

CHICKEN THIGHS WITH MUSHROOMS AND SUN-DRIED TOMATOES

SERVES 2

Sun-dried tomatoes are yet another flavor-packed ingredient useful in slow cooking. Here with the chicken and mushrooms, the tomatoes add a deep and slightly tart dimension in flavor, along with a little color. Avoid using the sun-dried tomatoes packed in oil, as they don't incorporate well and will make the dish too oily overall.

4 bone-in, skinless chicken thighs
Salt
Freshly ground black pepper
1 pound fresh mushrooms, sliced
¼ cup julienne cut sun-dried tomatoes
¼ cup chicken broth
¼ cup dry white wine
Chopped fresh or freeze-dried parsley, optional

1. Coat the inside of a 3½-quart slow cooker with cooking spray, if desired.

2. Sprinkle chicken thighs liberally with salt and pepper. Transfer to slow cooker.

3. Add the mushrooms and sun-dried tomatoes. Pour in broth and wine.

4. Cover and cook on High for 4 hours.

5. Taste, and season again with salt and pepper. Serve chicken with sauce and top with chopped parsley, if desired.

CACCIATORE-STYLE CHICKEN THIGHS
SERVES 2

Italian in origin, chicken cacciatore is also known as hunter's stew. It's a classic braised dish, perfect for the slow cooker, and produces tender, flavorful chicken.

½ small onion, sliced

½ red or green bell pepper, cored, seeded, and sliced

4 bone-in, skinless chicken thighs

Salt

Freshly ground black pepper

1 clove garlic, minced, or ½ teaspoon bottled minced garlic

¼ cup chicken broth or dry white wine

1 (14½-ounce) can diced tomatoes

½ teaspoon chopped fresh oregano, or ¼ teaspoon dried oregano

1 teaspoon chopped fresh basil, or ¼ teaspoon dried basil

Chopped fresh or freeze-dried parsley, optional

1. Coat the inside of a 3½-quart slow cooker with cooking spray, if desired.

2. Add the onion and bell pepper to slow cooker.

3. Sprinkle chicken thighs liberally with salt and pepper. Transfer to slow cooker on top of the onion mixture.

4. Add the garlic, broth or wine, tomatoes, and herbs.

5. Cover and cook on High for 4 hours.

6. Taste, and season again with salt and pepper. Serve chicken with sauce and top with chopped parsley, if desired.

MEDITERRANEAN CHICKEN

SERVES 2

The Silver Palate Cookbook defined the 1980s with completely new recipes and tastes, and home cooks everywhere adopted its recipes into their regular repertoire. Chicken Marbella was one of my favorites, which I adapted for my book, *The One-Armed Cook,* and adapt here once again for the slow cooker. Marinating the dish overnight dramatically improves the flavor, so plan ahead for it. Pour any remaining juices into a bowl to pass at the table.

1 clove garlic, minced, or $1/2$ teaspoon
   bottled minced garlic
1 tablespoon dried oregano
$1/2$ teaspoon salt
$1/4$ teaspoon freshly ground black pepper
3 tablespoons red wine vinegar
3 tablespoons olive oil
12 bite-sized pitted prunes
3 ounces pitted Spanish green olives
1 tablespoon capers, drained
1 bay leaf
4 bone-in, skinless chicken thighs
3 tablespoons light or dark brown sugar
3 tablespoons dry white wine

1. Combine the garlic, oregano, salt, pepper, vinegar, olive oil, prunes, green olives, capers, and bay leaf in a large resealable plastic bag. Shake well to mix. Add chicken thighs and turn to coat in the marinade. Refrigerate overnight, or at least several hours.

2. When ready to cook, coat the inside of a $3^{1}/2$-quart slow cooker with cooking spray, if desired.

3. Transfer chicken and its marinade to slow cooker. Stir the brown sugar and white wine together in a small bowl and pour over chicken.

4. Cover and cook on High for 4 hours.

5. Remove and discard bay leaf. Taste, and season again with salt and pepper. Serve chicken with the fruit and juices.

HONEY GINGER CHICKEN THIGHS

SERVES 2

Fresh ginger perks up any dish and adds a little savory to the sweetness of the honey. Coat a measuring cup with cooking spray and the honey will glide right out.

4 bone-in, skinless chicken thighs
Salt
Freshly ground black pepper
1/2 small onion, sliced
1 clove garlic, minced, or 1/2 teaspoon bottled minced garlic
1 teaspoon grated fresh ginger, or 1/2 teaspoon ground ginger
1/4 cup honey
1/4 cup ketchup

1. Coat the inside of a 3 1/2-quart slow cooker with cooking spray, if desired.

2. Sprinkle the chicken thighs liberally with salt and pepper. Transfer to slow cooker.

3. Stir together the onion, garlic, ginger, honey, and ketchup in a small bowl and pour over chicken thighs.

4. Cover and cook on High for 4 hours.

5. Taste, and season again with salt and pepper. Serve chicken with sauce.

FIVE-SPICE CHICKEN THIGHS

SERVES 2

These chicken thighs are just the right blend of spicy and sweet.

4 bone-in, skinless chicken thighs
2 tablespoons soy sauce
2 tablespoons dry sherry
2 tablespoons hoisin sauce
1 clove garlic, minced, or $1/2$ teaspoon
   bottled minced garlic
1 teaspoon grated fresh ginger, or
   $1/2$ teaspoon ground ginger
$1/2$ teaspoon Chinese five-spice powder

1. Coat the inside of a $3^1/2$-quart slow cooker with cooking spray, if desired.

2. Transfer the chicken thighs to slow cooker.

3. Stir together the soy sauce, sherry, hoisin sauce, garlic, ginger, and five-spice powder in a small bowl and pour over chicken thighs.

4. Cover and cook on High for 4 hours.

5. Taste, and season again with salt and pepper. Serve chicken with sauce.

ASIAN CHICKEN WINGS

SERVES 2

These wings can be an appetizer to share, or a dinner for two. The easiest way to grate the fresh ginger is to use a microplane grater.

$1^1/_2$ **pounds chicken wings, wing tips removed if desired**
$^1/_2$ **cup light or dark brown sugar**
$^1/_4$ **cup soy sauce**
$^1/_4$ **cup ketchup**
$^1/_2$ **cup hoisin sauce**
1 teaspoon grated fresh ginger, or $^1/_2$ teaspoon ground ginger
1 garlic clove, minced, or $^1/_2$ teaspoon bottled minced garlic
3 tablespoons dry sherry
2 green onions, white and some green part, thinly sliced
2 tablespoons toasted sesame seeds

1. Coat the inside of a $3^1/_2$-quart slow cooker with cooking spray, if desired.

2. Transfer the chicken wings to slow cooker.

3. Stir together the brown sugar, soy sauce, ketchup, hoisin sauce, ginger, garlic, and sherry in a small bowl; pour over wings. Stir well to mix and coat wings thoroughly.

4. Cover and cook on Low for 4 hours.

5. Remove to serving dish. Taste, and season again with salt and pepper. Top with green onions and sesame seeds.

STICKY WINGS
SERVES 2

Full-flavored and sticky, extra napkins will certainly be in order with these wings.

1 1/2 pounds chicken wings, wing tips removed if desired
Salt
Freshly ground black pepper
1/2 (6-ounce) can frozen orange juice concentrate
2 tablespoons port wine
1/4 cup honey
1 teaspoon grated fresh ginger, or 1/2 teaspoon ground ginger
Dash of cayenne pepper

1. Coat the inside of a 3 1/2-quart slow cooker with cooking spray, if desired.

2. Sprinkle the chicken wings liberally with salt and pepper. Transfer the chicken wings to slow cooker.

3. Stir together the orange juice concentrate, port wine, honey, ginger, and cayenne to taste in a small bowl and pour over chicken wings. Stir well to mix and coat wings thoroughly.

4. Cover and cook on Low for 4 hours.

5. Remove to serving dish. Taste, and season again with salt and pepper. And pass the napkins.

CHICKEN MEATBALLS

SERVES 2

Here's a one-pot meal of chicken meatballs on a bed of tomato-sauced rice. The ground chicken makes for a lighter, but still tasty, meatball.

1/4 cup seasoned breadcrumbs
1 tablespoon milk
1 (8-ounce) can tomato sauce
1 clove garlic, minced, or 1/2 teaspoon
    bottled minced garlic
1 teaspoon chopped fresh basil, or
    1/2 teaspoon dried basil
1/2 cup chicken broth
1/2 cup uncooked converted rice
1/2 pound ground chicken
Salt
Freshly ground black pepper

1. Coat the inside of a 3 1/2-quart slow cooker with cooking spray, if desired.

2. Stir together the breadcrumbs and milk in a small bowl and set aside.

3. Add the tomato sauce, garlic, basil, chicken broth, and rice to the slow cooker. Stir well to mix.

4. Add the chicken to the breadcrumb mixture. Season with salt and pepper. Mix together thoroughly, and form into 1-inch balls (about 10). Transfer meatballs to the slow cooker, on top of tomato-sauced rice.

5. Cover and cook on High for 1 1/2 hours. Check the temperature of a meatball with an instant-read thermometer. It should register 165 degrees. If not, cover and cook an additional 20 to 30 minutes.

6. Taste, and season again with salt and pepper. Serve in bowls.

GROUND TURKEY CHILI

SERVES 2+

Chili is a dish the slow cooker does really well, allowing the spices to meld and thoroughly flavor the meat. Use your own favorite chili spices if you prefer. Don't hesitate to stir this chili once during cooking.

1 pound ground turkey breast
$1/4$ cup chopped onion
1 clove garlic, minced, or $1/2$ teaspoon bottled minced garlic
$1/2$ (15-ounce) can dark kidney beans, rinsed and drained
1 cup chopped fresh tomatoes, or 1 ($14^1/2$-ounce) can diced tomatoes
1 teaspoon chili powder, or to taste
1 teaspoon ground cumin
$1/2$ teaspoon dried oregano
Chopped fresh cilantro, optional

1. Coat the inside of a $3^1/2$-quart slow cooker with cooking spray, if desired.

2. Transfer turkey to slow cooker and break apart the meat with the side of a spoon or edge of a spatula. Add remaining ingredients, except cilantro, to slow cooker and stir well to mix.

3. Cover and cook on Low for 7 to 8 hours.

4. Top with cilantro, if desired, before serving.

TURKEY MEATLOAF WITH BASIL AND MOZZARELLA

SERVES 2

This Italian-flavored meatloaf is less dense made with ground turkey, so if neat slices are desired, chill the finished loaf, cut into slices, and reheat. Using ground turkey breast makes a leaner meatloaf, but regular ground turkey works just fine as well. Building an aluminum foil "sling" for the slow cooker makes removing the meatloaf a breeze (see page 13). Fresh basil is almost imperative.

1/4 cup sun-dried tomatoes, chopped
1/4 cup ketchup
1/4 cup seasoned breadcrumbs
1/4 cup finely chopped onion
1 clove garlic, minced, or 1/2 teaspoon bottled minced garlic
1/4 cup fresh basil, chopped, or 1 tablespoon dried basil
1/4 cup shredded mozzarella cheese
1 large egg white
Salt
Freshly ground black pepper
1/2 pound ground turkey breast
1 (8-ounce) can tomato sauce

1. Coat the inside of a 3 1/2-quart slow cooker with cooking spray and prepare the aluminum foil sling (see page 13).

2. Stir together the sun-dried tomatoes, ketchup, breadcrumbs, onion, garlic, basil, cheese, egg white, and salt and pepper to taste in a small bowl. Add ground turkey and combine well. Shape into a loaf and transfer to the center of the prepared slow cooker. Pour tomato sauce over meatloaf.

3. Cover and cook on High for 3 hours. The meatloaf is cooked when an instant-read thermometer inserted into the middle of the loaf registers 165 degrees.

4. Remove cover, turn off slow cooker, and allow meatloaf to rest 10 minutes. Gather the four strips of the sling toward the center and lift to remove the loaf to a serving platter. Slide meatloaf off the foil with a spatula or knife. Chill, if you desire clean slices, or slice roughly and serve immediately.

TURKEY LEGS

SERVES 2

We like turkey all year-round, and turkey legs are so easy to cook in a slow cooker. Putting a small ring of aluminum foil under the meaty end of each leg keeps the meat from direct contact with the cooker insert and prevents that portion from becoming dry and overcooked. Grab the leg with your hand to eat Renaissance-fair style, or remove the meat from the bone to add to other dishes. If only a three-pack of turkey legs is available, you can cook all three at one time and reserve the extra meat for another dish.

2 turkey legs
Salt
Freshly ground black pepper
3 sprigs fresh rosemary, optional

1. Coat the inside of a 3$\frac{1}{2}$-quart slow cooker with cooking spray, if desired. Make two small rings of crumpled aluminum foil, about 3 inches in diameter.

2. Sprinkle the turkey legs liberally with salt and pepper, then transfer to the slow cooker, meaty ends down and propped up on the foil rings. Add rosemary sprigs to slow cooker.

3. Cover and cook on Low for 6 hours.

4. As the skin does not become crispy, you may wish to remove it before serving.

CORNISH HEN IN PORT WINE AND FIG PRESERVES

SERVES 2

Cornish game hens are just the right size to serve two people and nestle into the slow cooker with ease. Port wine is an excellent ingredient for slow cookers, as it always provides a little richer color for the ingredients. Preserves, jams, and jellies are handy ingredients to create easy sauces for poultry and meats. For a darker skin, baste the hen during cooking with sauce from the bottom of the slow cooker.

1 Cornish game hen
Salt
Freshly ground black pepper
2 sprigs fresh rosemary
¼ cup fig preserves
¼ cup port wine

1. Coat the inside of a 3½-quart slow cooker with cooking spray, if desired.

2. Sprinkle the hen liberally with salt and pepper. Insert rosemary into cavity. Transfer hen to the slow cooker.

3. Stir together the fig preserves and port wine in a small bowl and pour over hen.

4. Cover and cook on High for 5 hours.

5. Taste, and season again with salt and pepper. Serve sauce over hen.

CORNISH HEN DIJON

SERVES 2

Mustard has a transformative quality when heated, bringing the tang to full flavor. Used here at the end of cooking by stirring it into the cooking liquid, it brightens the flavor of the hen, while the tarragon completes the dish. It's nearly impossible not to think of the South of France when you dig in.

$1/2$ **small onion, sliced**

1 medium carrot, chopped

1 rib celery, chopped

$1/2$ **cup white wine**

2 cloves garlic, minced, or 1 teaspoon bottled minced garlic

1 Cornish game hen

Salt

Freshly ground black pepper

2 tablespoons Dijon mustard

1 teaspoon chopped fresh tarragon, or $1/2$ teaspoon dried tarragon

1. Coat the inside of a $3^1/2$-quart slow cooker with cooking spray, if desired.

2. Add onion, carrot, and celery to slow cooker and stir in wine.

3. Insert garlic into cavity of Cornish game hen and sprinkle skin liberally with salt and pepper. Transfer to slow cooker.

4. Cover and cook on High for 5 hours.

5. Remove hen and vegetables to a serving platter and cover loosely with foil to keep warm.

6. Stir the mustard into the juices and leave slow cooker uncovered while the mustard heats for about 15 minutes. Stir in tarragon, taste, and season again with salt and pepper. Serve sauce over hen and vegetables.

BEEF AND LAMB

BRAISED SHORT RIBS

SERVES 2

Rich and wonderful, these short ribs are a fall-apart tender delight.

1 (8-ounce) can tomato sauce
1/2 cup red wine
1/4 cup chopped onion
1 teaspoon Worcestershire sauce
1 clove garlic, minced, or 1/2 teaspoon
    bottled minced garlic
1 tablespoon light or dark brown sugar
Salt
Freshly ground black pepper
2 pounds beef short ribs

1. Coat the inside of a 3 1/2-quart slow cooker with cooking spray, if desired.

2. Stir in tomato sauce, red wine, onion, Worcestershire sauce, garlic, and sugar.

3. Sprinkle short ribs liberally with salt and pepper and transfer the ribs into the sauce.

4. Cover and cook on High for 4 hours. Taste, and season again with salt and pepper. Serve hot.

BONELESS BEEF SHANKS
SERVES 2

A family favorite for years, the recipe has been adjusted for a meal for two. Deeply satisfying, it's a hearty dish to warm souls on a cold night.

$1/2$ cup beef broth
3 tablespoons tomato paste
$1/4$ cup chopped onion
$1/2$ cup sliced fresh mushrooms
1 cup fresh baby carrots
1 clove garlic, minced, or $1/2$ teaspoon
   bottled minced garlic
1 pound beef shanks, (boneless, if available)
Salt
Freshly ground black pepper
1 tablespoon cornstarch, optional
1 tablespoon water, optional
1 tablespoon lemon juice

1. Coat the inside of a $3^1/2$-quart slow cooker with cooking spray, if desired.

2. Stir in beef broth, tomato paste, onion, mushrooms, carrots, and garlic.

3. Sprinkle beef shanks liberally with salt and pepper and transfer shanks to the slow cooker. Stir well to coat the shanks with the sauce.

4. Cover and cook on Low for 5 hours. Remove beef shanks to a serving platter and cover to keep warm.

5. If a thicker sauce is desired, combine cornstarch and water in a small bowl. Stir into sauce. Turn slow cooker to High, leave uncovered, and cook an additional 15 minutes for sauce to thicken.

6. Stir in lemon juice. Taste, and season again with salt and pepper. Pour sauce over beef, and serve.

STUFFED MEATLOAF

SERVES 2

A lean ground beef works best for this recipe, inspired by my friend and cookbook author Rebecca Lang. If the small balls of fresh mozzarella are unavailable, sprinkle the layer with shredded mozzarella.

1 large egg
$1/4$ cup finely chopped onion
$1/4$ cup seasoned breadcrumbs
1 tablespoon ketchup
$1/2$ teaspoon Worcestershire sauce
Salt
Freshly ground pepper
$1/2$ pound ground beef
4 small balls fresh mozzarella
1 (8-ounce) can tomato sauce

1. Coat the inside of a $3^1/2$-quart slow cooker with cooking spray and prepare the aluminum foil sling (see page 13).

2. Beat the egg in a medium bowl. Stir in the onion, breadcrumbs, ketchup, Worcestershire sauce, and salt and pepper to taste in a small bowl. Add ground beef and combine well. Form into two 5 x 3-inch ovals. Transfer one oval to the center of the prepared slow cooker. Place the 4 mozzarella balls evenly down the center of the meat. Move the second oval on top of the mozzarella and press around the edges to seal. Pour tomato sauce over meatloaf.

3. Cover and cook on High for 3 hours. The meatloaf is cooked when an instant-read thermometer inserted into the middle of the loaf registers 165 degrees.

4. Remove cover, turn off slow cooker, and allow meatloaf to rest 10 minutes. Gather the four strips of the sling toward the center and lift to remove the loaf to a serving platter. Slide meatloaf off the foil with a spatula or knife. Serve warm.

STUFFED PEPPERS WITH MOZZARELLA

SERVES 2

The peppers provide their own single-serve dish in this Italian-inspired meal. Use your favorite bell pepper; I prefer red, but sometimes I'll make it with two different colors for variety. Substitute your favorite marinara sauce, if desired.

$1/2$ **pound ground beef**
$1/3$ **cup uncooked converted rice**
$1/4$ **cup finely shredded mozzarella cheese**
$1/4$ **cup finely chopped onion**
1 clove garlic, minced, or $1/2$ teaspoon bottled minced garlic
1 teaspoon chopped fresh or freeze-dried parsley
Salt
Freshly ground black pepper
2 medium bell peppers, tops cut off, cored and seeded
1 (8-ounce) can tomato sauce
$1/2$ **cup beef broth**
Grated or shredded Parmesan cheese, optional

1. Coat the inside of a $3^1/2$-quart slow cooker with cooking spray, if desired.

2. Stir together the beef, rice, mozzarella cheese, onion, garlic, parsley, and salt and pepper to taste in a small bowl.

3. Spoon the beef mixture into the peppers, filling them about $3/4$ full. Transfer to the slow cooker.

4. Pour tomato sauce over peppers and add broth to bottom of slow cooker.

5. Cover and cook on Low for 6 hours.

6. Top with Parmesan cheese before serving, if desired.

BEEF MEATBALLS
SERVES 2

Moist and tender, these meatballs don't dry out in the slow cooker.

1/4 cup quick-cooking (not instant) oatmeal
1/3 cup milk
1/2 small onion, finely chopped
Salt
Freshly ground black pepper
1/2 pound ground beef
1/3 cup ketchup
2 tablespoons water
1 tablespoon vinegar
1 teaspoon granulated sugar

1. Coat the inside of a 3 1/2-quart slow cooker with cooking spray, if desired.

2. Stir together the oatmeal and milk in a small bowl.

3. Add the onion, salt and pepper to taste, and the beef to the oatmeal mixture. Mix together thoroughly, and form into 1-inch round balls (about 10). Transfer the meatballs to the slow cooker.

4. Combine the ketchup, water, vinegar, and sugar in a small bowl and pour over meatballs.

5. Cover and cook on Low for 5 hours. Check the temperature of a meatball with an instant-read thermometer. It should register 165 degrees. If not, cover and cook an additional 20 to 30 minutes.

6. Serve in bowls with sauce.

SHERRY-BRAISED LAMB SHOULDER CHOPS

SERVES 2

The option to puree the liquid and vegetables after removing the lamb provides a nearly instant, thick sauce for the chops.

1 small onion, chopped
1 medium carrot, chopped
1 clove garlic, minced, or $1/2$ teaspoon
   bottled minced garlic
$1/2$ to 1 pound lamb shoulder chops
Salt
Freshly ground black pepper
$1/4$ cup dry sherry
$1/2$ cup chicken broth
1 bay leaf

1. Coat the inside of a $3^1/2$-quart slow cooker with cooking spray, if desired.

2. Add the onion, carrot, and garlic to the slow cooker.

3. Sprinkle the chops liberally with salt and pepper and transfer chops to the slow cooker on top of the vegetables.

4. Add sherry, broth, and bay leaf.

5. Cover and cook on Low for 5 hours.

6. Remove the chops to a serving platter and cover loosely with foil to keep warm. Discard the bay leaf. If desired, use an immersion blender to puree remaining liquid and vegetables. Taste, and season again with salt and pepper. Serve over chops.

MIDDLE EASTERN LAMB SHOULDER CHOPS
SERVES 2

Cumin and coriander perfume these chops and elevate this dish to the divine.

1 tablespoon olive oil
1 teaspoon ground cumin
1/2 teaspoon ground coriander
Salt
Freshly ground black pepper
1/2 to 1 pound lamb shoulder chops
1 clove garlic, chopped
1 small onion, chopped
1 (14 1/2-ounce) can diced tomatoes, drained

1. Coat the inside of a 3 1/2-quart slow cooker with cooking spray, if desired.

2. Stir together olive oil, cumin, and coriander in a large bowl.

3. Sprinkle the chops liberally with salt and pepper. Add chops to the bowl and stir to coat well. Transfer chops to slow cooker.

4. Add garlic, onion, and tomatoes to top of chops.

5. Cover and cook on Low for 5 hours.

6. Remove to a serving platter. Taste, and season again with salt and pepper, then serve.

ROSEMARY LAMB AND TOMATO STEW

SERVES 2

Woodsy rosemary complements the earthiness of the lamb. The acidic tomatoes and wine help to tenderize the lamb, enhancing the work of the slow cooker.

½ to 1 pound lamb, cut for stew
Salt
Freshly ground black pepper
1 (14½-ounce) can diced tomatoes, drained
2 cloves garlic, minced
2 sprigs fresh rosemary, or ½ teaspoon
    dried rosemary
3 tablespoons dry red wine, optional

1. Coat the inside of a 3½-quart slow cooker with cooking spray, if desired.

2. Sprinkle the lamb liberally with salt and pepper. Transfer to slow cooker.

3. Stir in tomatoes, garlic, rosemary, and red wine.

4. Cover and cook on Low for 5 hours.

5. Remove to a serving bowl. Taste, and season again with salt and pepper. Serve with rice or other grain.

DOUBLE DINNERS

BEEF BOTTOM ROUND

Carefully follow the preparation and finishing instructions to avoid getting burned from the hot food and liquids.

LINER #1—PEPPERY BOTTOM ROUND
SERVES 2

Worcestershire sauce is the key to the peppery flavor in the beef.

1/2 of a 2-pound bottom round roast
Salt
Freshly ground black pepper
1 small carrot, chopped
1 small onion, chopped
1 rib celery, chopped
2 tablespoons Worcestershire sauce
1/2 teaspoon garlic powder
4 sprigs fresh thyme, or 1/2 teaspoon dried thyme

1. Place round roast in the bottom of a slow cooker liner bag.

2. Sprinkle liberally with salt and pepper.

3. Add remaining ingredients, in order, to the bag on top of roast and set aside.

LINER #2 FALL-FLAVORED BOTTOM ROUND
SERVES 2

Dried fruit in port wine brings a subtle sweetness to the roast.

1/2 of a 2-pound bottom round roast
Salt
Freshly ground black pepper
1/2 cup mixed dried fruit, chopped, such as apricots, cranberries, and raisins
1 small onion, chopped
1/2 cup port wine

1. Place round roast in the bottom of a slow cooker liner bag.

2. Sprinkle liberally with salt and pepper.

3. Add remaining ingredients, in order, to the bag on top of roast and set aside.

TO COMPLETE THE RECIPE:

1. Place both liner bags, side by side, into the slow cooker. Drape each liner (closed) away from the other, extending over the sides of the slow cooker.

2. Cover and cook on Low for 6 hours.

3. Move two large, shallow serving dishes or bowls next to the slow cooker. Remove cover and using pot holders or oven mitts, carefully remove each liner and its contents to its own serving bowl. Let the liner rest open and allow contents to cool slightly. Remove the meat from the liner using tongs, and transfer to the serving bowl. Then grasp the bag, holding the top, and cut a corner off the bottom of the bag, large enough to allow the remaining contents of the bag to be released over the beef and into the bowl. Discard the liner. Repeat with the other dinner.

4. Allow the dinner not being served to cool, and package in a resealable plastic freezer bag or freezer container (remember to label it!).

5. Before serving, taste, and season again with salt and pepper.

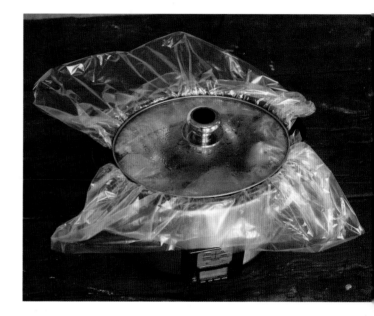

FLANK STEAK SOUTHWEST

Carefully follow the preparation and finishing instructions to avoid getting burned from the hot food and liquids.

LINER #1—SOUTHWESTERN FLANK STEAK WITH A LITTLE KICK
SERVES 2

Reminiscent of the classic Cuban dish Ropa Vieja. Shred meat with two forks if desired.

$1/2$ of a 1 to $1^1/2$-pound flank steak
Salt
Freshly ground black pepper
$1/2$ teaspoon chili powder, or more to taste
$1/2$ teaspoon freshly chopped oregano, or
   $1/4$ teaspoon dried oregano
1 small onion, thinly sliced
1 clove garlic, minced, or $1/2$ teaspoon bottled
   minced garlic
1 green bell pepper, cored, seeded and sliced
1 tablespoon fresh lime juice, or bottled lime juice
$1/2$ cup beef broth
1 (15-ounce) can black beans, rinsed and drained,
   optional

1. Place flank steak in the bottom of a slow cooker liner bag.

2. Sprinkle liberally with salt and pepper.

3. Add remaining ingredients on top of steak, and set aside.

LINER #2 FLANK STEAK FAJITA
SERVES 2

Serve this classic dish with tortillas, if desired.

$1/2$ of a 1 to $1^1/2$-pound flank steak
1 (4-ounce) can chopped green chiles
1 clove garlic, minced, or $1/2$ teaspoon bottled
   minced garlic
1 ($14^1/2$-ounce) can diced tomatoes
$1/2$ teaspoon chili powder
$1/4$ teaspoon cumin
1 tablespoon chopped fresh or freeze-dried parsley

1. Place flank steak in the bottom of a slow cooker liner bag.

2. Sprinkle liberally with salt and pepper.

3. Add remaining ingredients on top of steak, and set aside.

TO COMPLETE THE RECIPE:

1. Place both liner bags, side by side, into the slow cooker. Drape each liner (closed) away from the other, extending over the sides of the slow cooker.

2. Cover and cook on Low for 6 to 7 hours.

3. Move two large, shallow serving dishes or bowls next to the slow cooker. Remove cover and using pot holders or oven mitts, carefully remove each liner and its contents to its own serving bowl. Let the liner rest open and allow contents to cool slightly. Remove the meat from the liner using tongs, and transfer to the serving bowl. Then grasp the bag, holding the top, and cut a corner off the bottom of the bag, large enough to allow the remaining contents of the bag to be released over the beef and into the bowl. Discard the liner. Repeat with the other dinner.

4. Allow the dinner not being served to cool, and package in a resealable plastic freezer bag or freezer container (remember to label it!).

5. Before serving, taste, and season again with salt and pepper.

FLANK STEAK DRESSED UP

Carefully follow the preparation and finishing instructions to avoid getting burned from the hot food and liquids.

LINER #1—RED WINE FLANK STEAK
SERVES 2

This is my go-to marinade for steak.

$1/2$ **of a 1-1$1/2$ pound flank steak**
Salt
Freshly ground black pepper
$1/4$ **teaspoon crushed red pepper**
2 cloves garlic, minced, or 1 teaspoon bottled
   minced garlic
2 tablespoons fresh lemon juice, or bottled
   lemon juice
$3/4$ **cup dry red wine**
2 sprigs rosemary, or $1/2$ teaspoon dried
   rosemary, crushed

1. Place flank steak in the bottom of a slow cooker liner bag.

2. Sprinkle liberally with salt and pepper.

3. Add remaining ingredients on top of steak, and set aside.

LINER #2 STUFFED FLANK STEAK
SERVES 2

A truly special dish, it's worth the extra few minutes it takes to cut open the steak. Freezing the steak for about 20 minutes makes it easier to slice.

$1/2$ **of a 1-1$1/2$ pound flank steak**
2 tablespoons pesto sauce
3 tablespoons grated or shredded Parmesan
   cheese
$3/4$ **cup sliced fresh mushrooms**
Salt
Freshly ground black pepper
$1/4$ **cup beef broth**

1. Slice flank steak open like a book. Spread evenly with pesto sauce, sprinkle with Parmesan cheese, and top with mushrooms. Roll up steak from the long side and secure with wooden skewers or toothpicks.

2. Sprinkle outside of stuffed flank steak liberally with salt and pepper.

3. Place flank steak in the bottom of a slow cooker liner bag. Pour broth over steak, and set aside.

TO COMPLETE THE RECIPE:

1. Place both liner bags, side by side, into the slow cooker. Drape each liner (closed) away from the other, extending over the sides of the slow cooker.

2. Cover and cook on Low for 6 to 7 hours.

3. Move two large, shallow serving dishes or bowls next to the slow cooker. Remove cover and using pot

holders or oven mitts, carefully remove each liner and its contents to its own serving bowl. Let the liner rest open and allow contents to cool slightly. Remove the meat from the liner using tongs, and transfer to the serving bowl. Then grasp the bag, holding the top, and cut a corner off the bottom of the bag, large enough to allow the remaining contents of the bag to be released over the beef and into the bowl. Discard the liner. Repeat with the other dinner.

4. For the Stuffed Flank Steak, remove the skewer and slice before serving.

5. Allow the dinner not being served to cool, and package in a resealable plastic freezer bag or freezer container (remember to label it!).

6. Before serving, taste, and season again with salt and pepper.

STUFFED FLANK STEAK

POT ROAST

Carefully follow the preparation and finishing instructions to avoid getting burned from the hot food and liquids.

LINER #1—LIME POT ROAST WITH TOMATO SAUCE

SERVES 2

This is our all-time favorite pot roast recipe, originally hailing from my dear friend and co-author Nathalie Dupree from her timeless cookbook *New Southern Cooking*, and adapted here for the slow cooker.

1/2 of a 2–2 1/2 pound chuck roast
Salt
Freshly ground black pepper
Grated rind of 1 lime, no white attached
3 tablespoons fresh lime juice, or bottled lime juice
2 cloves garlic, minced, or 1 teaspoon bottled minced garlic
1 cup beef broth
1/2 teaspoon dried Italian seasoning
1 (14 1/2-ounce) can crushed tomatoes

1. Place chuck roast in the bottom of a slow cooker liner bag.

2. Sprinkle liberally with salt and pepper.

3. Add remaining ingredients, in order, to the bag on top of roast and set aside.

LINER #2 VINEGAR-BRAISED POT ROAST

SERVES 2

The coffee deepens the flavors in this dish, producing a rich, delicious roast.

1/2 of a 2–2 1/2 pound chuck roast
Salt
Freshly ground black pepper
1 small onion, sliced
1/2 cup strong coffee
1 tablespoon balsamic vinegar
2 sprigs rosemary, or 1/2 teaspoon dried rosemary, crushed

1. Place chuck roast in the bottom of a slow cooker liner bag.

2. Sprinkle liberally with salt and black pepper.

3. Add remaining ingredients on top of roast and set aside.

TO COMPLETE THE RECIPE:

1. Place both liner bags, side by side, into the slow cooker. Drape each liner (closed) away from the other, extending over the sides of the slow cooker.

2. Cover and cook on Low for 8 hours.

3. Move two large, shallow serving dishes or bowls next to the slow cooker. Remove cover and using pot holders or oven mitts, carefully remove each liner and its contents to its own serving bowl. Let the liner rest open and allow contents to cool slightly. Remove the meat from the liner using tongs, and transfer to the serving bowl. Then grasp the bag, holding the top, and cut a corner off the bottom of the bag, large enough to allow the remaining contents of the bag to be released over the beef and into the bowl. Discard the liner. Repeat with the other dinner.

4. Allow the dinner not being served to cool, and package in a resealable plastic freezer bag or freezer container (remember to label it!).

5. Before serving, taste, and season again with salt and pepper.

POT ROAST WITH A TWIST

Carefully follow the preparation and finishing instructions to avoid getting burned from the hot food and liquids.

LINER #1—SWEET TOMATO POT ROAST
SERVES 2

Do use the fresh ginger if at all possible for this roast. It balances the sweetness of the dish.

$1/2$ of a 2-2$1/2$ pound chuck roast
Salt
Freshly ground black pepper
$1/2$ cup cranberry juice
1 (8-ounce) can tomato sauce
1 tablespoon vinegar
1 small onion, chopped
1 teaspoon freshly grated ginger, or $1/2$ teaspoon ground ginger
1 teaspoon ground cinnamon

1. Place chuck roast in the bottom of a slow cooker liner bag.

2. Sprinkle liberally with salt and pepper.

3. Stir together the cranberry juice, tomato sauce, vinegar, onion, ginger, and cinnamon in a small bowl. Pour over roast, and set aside.

LINER #2 HORSERADISH POT ROAST WITH VEGETABLES
SERVES 2

The kick from the horseradish in this recipe gives the roast a subtle bite.

$1/2$ of a 2-2$1/2$ pound chuck roast
Salt
Freshly ground black pepper
1 small baking potato, peeled and cut into $1/2$-inch chunks
1 medium carrot, cut into $1/2$-inch chunks
1 small onion, chopped
1 cup beef broth
1 tablespoon vinegar
1 tablespoon ketchup
1 tablespoon prepared horseradish
1 tablespoon Dijon mustard
1 teaspoon granulated sugar

1. Place chuck roast in the bottom of a slow cooker liner bag.

2. Sprinkle liberally with salt and pepper.

3. Top with potato, carrot, and onion. Stir together broth, vinegar, ketchup, horseradish, mustard, and sugar. Pour over roast and set aside.

TO COMPLETE THE RECIPE:

1. Place both liner bags, side by side, into the slow cooker. Drape each liner (closed) away from the other, extending over the sides of the slow cooker.

2. Cover and cook on Low for 8 hours.

3. Move two large, shallow serving dishes or bowls next to the slow cooker. Remove cover and using pot holders or oven mitts, carefully remove each liner and its contents to its own serving bowl. Let the liner rest open and allow contents to cool slightly. Remove the meat from the liner using tongs, and transfer to the serving bowl. Then grasp the bag, holding the top, and cut a corner off the bottom of the bag, large enough to allow the remaining contents of the bag to be released over the beef and into the bowl. Discard the liner. Repeat with the other dinner.

4. Allow the dinner not being served to cool, and package in a resealable plastic freezer bag or freezer container (remember to label it!).

5. Before serving, taste, and season again with salt and pepper.

PORK TENDERLOIN

Carefully follow the preparation and finishing instructions to avoid getting burned from the hot food and liquids.

LINER #1—PARMESAN-CRUSTED PORK TENDERLOIN
SERVES 2

This pork emerges perfectly moist and tender.

$1/2$ of a 1-pound pork tenderloin
Salt
Freshly ground black pepper
$1/4$ cup honey
1 tablespoon soy sauce
1 tablespoon dried basil or chives
1 clove garlic, minced, or $1/2$ teaspoon bottled
   minced garlic
1 tablespoon olive oil
$1/3$ cup grated or shredded Parmesan cheese

1. Place pork tenderloin in the bottom of a slow cooker liner bag.

2. Sprinkle liberally with salt and pepper.

3. Stir together the honey, soy sauce, basil, garlic, and olive oil in a small bowl. Pour over tenderloin, sprinkle with Parmesan cheese, and set aside.

LINER #2 BBQ PORK TENDERLOIN
SERVES 2

Here's a classic barbecue preparation. If pressed for time, just coat the tenderloin in your favorite barbecue sauce.

$1/2$ of a 1 pound pork tenderloin
Salt
Freshly ground black pepper
$1/2$ cup ketchup
2 tablespoons light or dark brown sugar
1 tablespoon vinegar
1 teaspoon Dijon mustard
1 tablespoon soy sauce
$1/2$ teaspoon chili powder
1 clove garlic, minced, or $1/2$ teaspoon bottled
   minced garlic
$1/2$ teaspoon onion powder

1. Place pork tenderloin in the bottom of a slow cooker liner bag.

2. Sprinkle liberally with salt and pepper.

3. Stir together the ketchup, brown sugar, vinegar, Dijon mustard, soy sauce, chili powder, garlic, and onion powder in a small bowl. Pour over tenderloin, and set aside.

TO COMPLETE THE RECIPE:

1. Place both liner bags, side by side, into the slow cooker. Drape each liner (closed) away from the other, extending over the sides of the slow cooker.

2. Cover and cook on Low for 6 hours.

3. Move two large, shallow serving dishes or bowls next to the slow cooker. Remove cover and using pot holders or oven mitts, carefully remove each liner and its contents to its own serving bowl. Let the liner rest open and allow contents to cool slightly. Remove the tenderloin from the liner using tongs, and transfer to the serving bowl. Then grasp the bag, holding the top, and cut a corner off the bottom of the bag, large enough to allow the remaining contents of the bag to be released over the pork and into the bowl. Discard the liner. Repeat with the other dinner.

4. Allow the dinner not being served to cool, and package in a resealable plastic freezer bag or freezer container (remember to label it!).

5. Before serving, taste, and season again with salt and pepper.

PARMESAN-CRUSTED PORK TENDERLOIN

PORK TENDERLOIN WITH SPICES

Carefully follow the preparation and finishing instructions to avoid getting burned from the hot food and liquids.

LINER #1—PORK TENDERLOIN WITH CABBAGE

SERVES 2

The tenderloin stays moist, using very little liquid, with the cabbage acting as a shield to keep the moisture in.

1/2 of a 1-pound pork tenderloin
1/4 cup water
Salt
Freshly ground black pepper
1 teaspoon cumin
1 teaspoon garlic powder
1 teaspoon dried basil
1 small carrot, chopped
1 small onion, chopped
1/2 (8-ounce) bag shredded cabbage
1/2 teaspoon fennel seed

1. Place pork tenderloin and water in the bottom of a slow cooker liner bag.

2. Sprinkle liberally with salt and pepper.

3. Sprinkle cumin, garlic powder, and basil over tenderloin. Top with carrot, onion, cabbage, and fennel seed. Set aside.

LINER #2 JERK PORK TENDERLOIN

SERVES 2

The rich spices of allspice, cinnamon, ginger, and cloves help to give this tenderloin its deep flavor.

1 cup beef broth
1 teaspoon onion powder
1 teaspoon garlic powder
1 teaspoon crushed red pepper
1/4 teaspoon allspice
1/4 teaspoon ground cinnamon
1/4 teaspoon ground ginger
1/8 teaspoon ground cloves
1/2 of a 1-pound pork tenderloin

1. Add beef broth to the bottom of a slow cooker liner bag and set aside.

2. Stir together the dried onions, garlic powder, red pepper flakes, allspice, cinnamon, ginger, and cloves in a small bowl. Rub into tenderloin, transfer to broth in liner bag, and set aside.

TO COMPLETE THE RECIPE:

1. Place both liner bags, side by side, into the slow cooker. Drape each liner (closed) away from the other, extending over the sides of the slow cooker.

2. Cover and cook on Low for 6 hours.

3. Move two large, shallow serving dishes or bowls next to the slow cooker. Remove cover and using pot holders or oven mitts, carefully remove each liner and its contents to its own serving bowl. Let the liner rest open and allow contents to cool slightly. Remove the tenderloin from the liner using tongs, and transfer to the serving bowl. Then grasp the bag, holding the top, and cut a corner off the bottom of the bag, large enough to allow it the remaining contents of the bag to be released over the pork and into the bowl. Discard the liner. Repeat with the other dinner.

4. Allow the dinner not being served to cool, and package in a resealable plastic freezer bag or freezer container (remember to label it!).

5. Before serving, taste, and season again with salt and pepper.

TURKEY TENDERLOIN

Carefully follow the preparation and finishing instructions to avoid getting burned from the hot food and liquids.

LINER #1—TURKEY BREAST TENDERLOIN WITH CRANBERRY-ORANGE SAUCE
SERVES 2

A taste of Thanksgiving just for two—any time of year.

2 pounds turkey breast tenderloins
Salt
Freshly ground black pepper
1/3 cup orange juice
3/4 cup whole cranberry sauce
2 tablespoons light or dark brown sugar
1 tablespoon soy sauce
1/2 teaspoon allspice

1. Place turkey breast tenderloin in the bottom of a slow cooker liner bag.

2. Sprinkle liberally with salt and pepper.

3. Stir together the orange juice, cranberry sauce, brown sugar, soy sauce, and allspice in a small bowl. Pour over tenderloin and set aside.

LINER #2 KALAMATA TURKEY TENDERLOIN WITH GREEK SEASONING
SERVES 2

Greek olives and oregano give this turkey its Mediterranean flair.

2 pounds turkey breast tenderloins
1/4 cup chicken broth
1 tablespoon fresh lemon juice, or bottled lemon juice
Salt
Freshly ground black pepper
1/4 teaspoon dried oregano
1/4 teaspoon dried basil
1/4 teaspoon garlic powder
1 small onion, chopped
1/2 cup pitted kalamata or other Greek-style olives
2 tablespoons chopped sun-dried tomatoes

1. Place turkey breast tenderloins, chicken broth, and lemon juice in the bottom of a slow cooker liner bag.

2. Sprinkle liberally with salt and pepper.

3. Sprinkle oregano, basil, and garlic powder over tenderloin. Top with onion, olives, and tomatoes, and set aside.

TO COMPLETE THE RECIPE:

1. Place both liner bags, side by side, into the slow cooker. Drape each liner (closed) away from the other, extending over the sides of the slow cooker.

2. Cover and cook on Low for 6 to 7 hours.

3. Move two large, shallow serving dishes or bowls next to the slow cooker. Remove cover and using pot holders or oven mitts, carefully remove each liner and its contents to its own serving bowl. Let the liner rest open and allow contents to cool slightly. Remove the tenderloins from the liner using tongs, and transfer to the serving bowl. Then grasp the bag, holding the top, and cut a corner off the bottom of the bag, large enough to allow the remaining contents of the bag to be released over the turkey and into the bowl. Discard the liner. Repeat with the other dinner.

4. Allow the dinner not being served to cool, and package in a resealable plastic freezer bag or freezer container (remember to label it!).

5. Before serving, taste, and season again with salt and pepper.

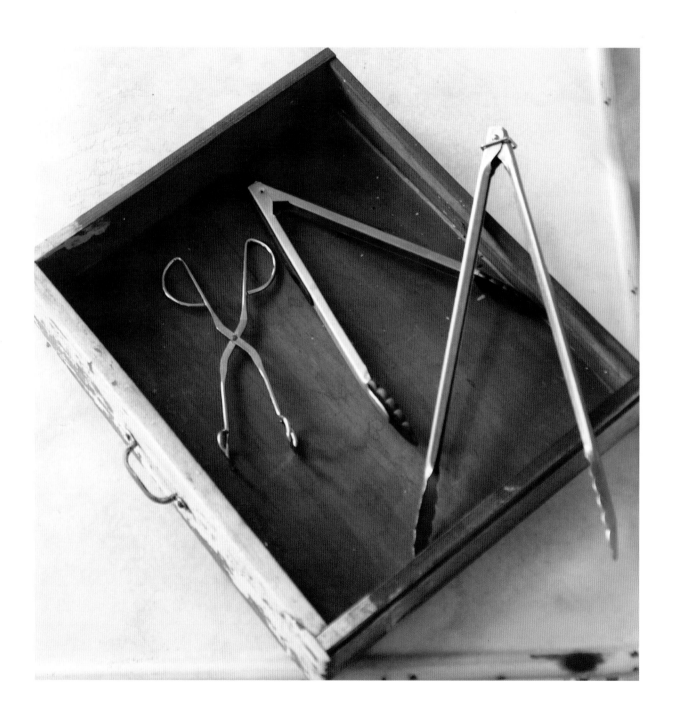

SEAFOOD

FOIL-POUCH LEMON-DILL SALMON
SERVES 2

The short cooking time for this dish makes it a candidate for an after-work preparation. Cooking in a foil pouch not only leaves you with a nearly clean slow cooker, but it helps to keep the salmon incredibly moist. This basic preparation with lemon and dill will inspire you to be creative and try new flavor combinations—maybe diced tomatoes and tarragon.

2 salmon fillets
1 teaspoon snipped fresh dill, or $1/2$ teaspoon dried dill
4–6 slices of fresh lemon, plus additional lemon, if desired
Salt
Freshly ground black pepper

1. Transfer the salmon to the center of a large sheet of aluminum foil. Sprinkle dill evenly over both fillets. Cover the fillets with lemon slices. Close the aluminum foil by folding the ends over to form a pouch. Move the pouch to the slow cooker.

2. Cover and cook on Low for 2 hours. Carefully remove pouch to a serving plate. Uncover to let steam escape. Season to taste with salt and pepper. Serve with additional lemon, if desired.

SHRIMP IN HERB BUTTER SAUCE

SERVES 2

Shrimp cooks very quickly in a slow cooker, so the majority of time involved for this recipe is to allow the sauce flavors to mellow together. Also try this recipe using just butter and seafood seasoning. Pass the napkins!

6 tablespoons butter, room temperature
1 clove garlic, minced, or 1/2 teaspoon bottled minced garlic
2 sprigs fresh thyme, or 1/2 teaspoon dried thyme
Pinch of red pepper flakes, optional
1 tablespoon lemon juice
1 pound large shrimp, peeled and deveined
Chopped fresh or freeze-dried parsley, or other fresh or dried herb

1. Coat the inside of a 3$\frac{1}{2}$-quart slow cooker with cooking spray, if desired.

2. Add butter, garlic, thyme, red pepper flakes if using, and lemon juice to slow cooker.

3. Cover and cook on Low for 2 hours. Remove lid and add shrimp; turn slow cooker to High.

4. Cook shrimp 20 to 30 minutes in the butter sauce, until the shrimp is fully pink throughout and no longer translucent. Remove to serving bowl, sprinkle with parsley or other herb, and serve with French bread.

SIDE DISHES

BAKED POTATOES

SERVES 2

Whether there isn't an available oven, or it's just too hot to have the oven on, these crock-baked potatoes are the answer.

2 baking potatoes
1 tablespoon olive oil
Salt
Freshly ground black pepper

1. Coat the inside of a $3^1/_2$-quart slow cooker with cooking spray, if desired.

2. Rub outside of potatoes with olive oil and place in slow cooker. Sprinkle liberally with salt and pepper.

3. Cover and cook on High for 3 to 4 hours. Serve with the usual accompaniments.

CROCKED RED POTATOES WITH PARMESAN

SERVES 2

Make this recipe your own by selecting your favorite fresh or dried herbs to change the flavor of these potatoes.

1 pound red or new potatoes, cut into wedges
$1/2$ small onion, chopped
1 tablespoon chopped fresh basil, or
    1 teaspoon dried basil
Salt
Freshly ground black pepper
$1/2$ cup grated or shredded Parmesan cheese

1. Coat the inside of a $3^1/2$-quart slow cooker with cooking spray, if desired.

2. Add potato wedges to slow cooker. Stir in onion and basil. Sprinkle liberally with salt and pepper.

3. Cover and cook on High for 4 hours. Remove to serving dish and top with grated Parmesan cheese.

POTATO GRATIN WITH FRESH HERBS

SERVES 2+

Potatoes in the slow cooker are a boon to the cook. The potatoes soften to the perfect texture for eating and soak up the flavor of the fresh herbs. While a mandolin makes easy work of slicing the potatoes, it also makes easy work of slicing a finger. Be careful if you use one.

1 pound baking potatoes, peeled and thinly sliced
1 clove garlic, minced, or $1/2$ teaspoon bottled minced garlic
1 tablespoon chopped fresh or freeze-dried parsley
2 teaspoons chopped fresh or freeze-dried chives
$1/2$ teaspoon chopped fresh thyme, or a pinch of dried thyme
1 tablespoon olive oil
Salt
Freshly ground black pepper
$1/2$ cup grated or shredded Parmesan cheese, divided

1. Coat the inside of a $3^1/2$-quart slow cooker with cooking spray, if desired.

2. Toss the potato slices in a large bowl with the garlic, parsley, chives, thyme, and olive oil. Sprinkle liberally with salt and pepper. Transfer the potatoes to slow cooker. Add all at once, or arrange in a spiral pattern in layers. If layering, add 1 tablespoon of the Parmesan cheese to each of the layers. If not layering, add 2 tablespoons of the Parmesan cheese when tossing with the herbs.

3. Cover and cook on High for 6 hours. Remove to serving dish and top with remaining Parmesan cheese.

MASHED POTATOES WITH CHEESE

SERVES 2

Mashed potatoes are so easy in the slow cooker and you never have to worry about the pot boiling over on the stove!

2 large baking potatoes, peeled and cut into
    $1/2$-inch dice
$1/4$ cup chicken broth
Salt
Freshly ground black pepper
$1/2$ cup shredded cheese (Cheddar, Mexican
    blend, crumbled feta, or goat)
1 teaspoon chopped fresh herbs (chives, dill,
    parsley, or your favorite)
2 tablespoons butter, room temperature

1. Coat the inside of a $3^1/2$-quart slow cooker with cooking spray, if desired.

2. Transfer the potatoes and broth to the slow cooker. Sprinkle liberally with salt and pepper.

3. Cover and cook on High for 6 hours, stirring once or twice during cooking, if possible. This prevents the potatoes from turning dark.

4. Mash the potatoes while still warm using a hand potato masher. Stir in cheese, herbs, and butter. Taste, and season again with salt and pepper. Serve hot.

CARROTS IN PORT WINE

The port wine and beef broth bring out a heartier flavor in these carrots.

1 tablespoon butter, room temperature
1/4 cup beef broth
1/4 cup port wine
1 tablespoon light or dark brown sugar
1 (16-ounce) bag fresh baby carrots

1. Coat the inside of a 3 1/2-quart slow cooker with cooking spray, if desired.

2. Turn the slow cooker on High and add the butter. When butter has melted, add the broth, port wine, and brown sugar. Stir well to mix. Add the carrots and stir to coat in the sauce. Turn the slow cooker to Low.

3. Cover and cook on Low for 4 hours, until carrots are tender. Serve hot.

GLAZED CARROTS

SERVES 2

Carrots have a natural affinity with oranges. The orange marmalade provides a shiny glaze for the carrots and the tarragon balances the sweetness.

3 tablespoons butter, room temperature
1/3 cup orange marmalade
1/2 tablespoon chopped fresh tarragon, or
   1/2 teaspoon dried tarragon
1/4 cup chicken broth
1 (16-ounce) bag fresh baby carrots

1. Coat the inside of a 3 1/2-quart slow cooker with cooking spray, if desired.

2. Turn the slow cooker on High and add the butter and marmalade. When butter has melted, stir and add the tarragon, and chicken broth. Stir well to mix. Add the carrots and stir to coat in the sauce. Turn the slow cooker to Low.

3. Cover and cook on Low for 4 hours, until carrots are tender. Serve hot.

BAKED SWEET POTATOES
SERVES 2

Packed with nutrition, high in fiber, and naturally sweet, these jewels are a welcome alternative to regular potatoes. Serve hot with lots of butter—and maybe a dash of cinnamon-sugar.

2 sweet potatoes
Salt
Freshly ground black pepper

1. Coat the inside of a 3$^{1}/_{2}$-quart slow cooker with cooking spray, if desired.

2. Prick the potatoes all over with a fork or the tip of a sharp knife. Sprinkle liberally with salt and pepper.

3. Cover and cook on Low for 5 to 6 hours.

MASHED SWEET POTATOES

SERVES 2

All through the winter, sweet potatoes are "in season" and add bright color to a dinner plate. These mashed sweet potatoes are as good as it gets.

1/2 to 1 pound sweet potatoes, peeled and cut into 1/2-inch slices
1/2 cup apple or cranberry juice, divided
1/2 teaspoon ground cinnamon
1/4 teaspoon ground nutmeg
1/4 teaspoon allspice
1/4 teaspoon ground cloves
Butter, optional
1/4 cup chopped pecans, optional

1. Coat the inside of a 3 1/2-quart slow cooker with cooking spray, if desired.

2. Add the sweet potatoes and 1/4 cup of the juice to slow cooker. Sprinkle in cinnamon, nutmeg, allspice, and cloves. Stir well to mix.

3. Cover and cook on Low for 5 hours. Using a hand potato masher or an immersion blender, mash the potatoes until desired consistency, adding remaining juice as needed for a smooth texture. Stir in butter to taste, and pecans, if desired. Serve hot.

ROASTED ROOT VEGETABLES

SERVES 2+

This standard side dish is a blank slate for creativity. Add any seasonings you desire to make this recipe your own. Even prepared simply as below, these root vegetables are tasty and satisfying.

$1/2$ **pound potatoes (such as new, or bakers), peeled and cut into 1-inch dice**

$1/2$ **pound turnips, peeled and cut into 1-inch dice**

1 medium carrot, cut into 1-inch dice

2 shallots, peeled and cut into slices

2 cloves garlic, minced, or $1/2$ teaspoon bottled minced garlic

1 tablespoon butter, room temperature

Salt

Freshly ground black pepper

1 tablespoon chopped fresh or freeze-dried chives

1. Coat the inside of a $3^1/2$-quart slow cooker with cooking spray, if desired.

2. Add the potatoes, turnips, carrot, shallots, garlic, and butter to slow cooker. Sprinkle liberally with salt and pepper. Stir well to mix.

3. Cover and cook on High for 4 hours. Check vegetables for tenderness. Cook additional 30 to 60 minutes to insure tenderness.

4. Remove vegetables to a serving dish. Taste, season again with salt and pepper, and sprinkle with chives.

POLENTA

SERVES 2+

Polenta can be a blank slate for almost anything. We enjoy it topped with a marinara sauce, or with leftover meats and/or vegetables mixed in.

3/4 cup stone-ground yellow cornmeal
1 1/2 cups chicken broth
1 1/2 cups water
1/4 cup grated or shredded cheese (such as Parmesan, Swiss, or mozzarella)
1 tablespoon butter, room temperature
Salt
Freshly ground black pepper

1. Coat the inside of a 3 1/2-quart slow cooker with cooking spray or insert a disposable liner, both optional.

2. Add cornmeal, chicken broth, and water. Stir well to mix.

3. Cover and cook on High for 2 hours. Stir and then continue to cook for an additional 30 minutes. Stir in cheese and butter, season to taste with salt and pepper, and serve hot.

CORN PUDDING

SERVES 2+

Warm, soft spoonfuls of corn pudding go well with almost any meat. It's even nice for lunch or an afternoon snack. Always wear gloves when chopping fresh peppers. Canned diced jalapenos also work well in this recipe. Note the two stages of cooking time.

1 tablespoon butter, room temperature
1 tablespoon all-purpose flour
$1/2$ teaspoon baking powder
Pinch of salt
$1/2$ cup milk
1 large egg, lightly beaten
1 cup fresh or frozen corn kernels, thawed
  if frozen
2 teaspoons chopped jalapeno pepper
$1/4$ cup shredded cheese (Cheddar, Mexican,
  or other favorite)

1. Coat the inside of a $3^{1}/_{2}$-quart slow cooker with cooking spray, if desired.

2. Melt butter on High in the slow cooker.

3. Whisk the flour, baking powder, and salt together in a small bowl and stir in the milk, egg, corn, and pepper. Transfer to slow cooker on top of the melted butter. Stir in cheese. Change the heat setting to Low.

4. Cover and cook on Low for 3 hours. Serve warm.

GRITS CASSEROLE

SERVES 2+

Stone-ground grits are far superior to commonly found grocery store grits. The deep, almost nutty flavor is enhanced when the grits are cooked in broth. This side dish isn't just for brunch: it's marvelous as a bed under pork chops or shrimp. Note the two-step cooking time, for a total of 5 hours.

2 tablespoons butter, room temperature
$^1/_2$ cup stone-ground grits
$1^1/_2$ cups chicken broth
2 large eggs, slightly beaten
$^1/_4$ cup heavy cream
1 cup shredded Cheddar cheese, or freshly
   grated or shredded Parmesan cheese
Salt
Freshly ground black pepper

1. Coat the inside of a $3^1/_2$-quart slow cooker with cooking spray or insert a disposable liner, both optional.

2. Turn slow cooker on High and add butter. When butter is melted, add grits and chicken broth to slow cooker, stirring well to mix. Reduce the cooking temperature to Low.

3. Cover and cook on Low for 3 hours. Stir in eggs, cream, and cheese, and continue to cook on Low for 2 hours.

4. Taste, and season again with salt and pepper. Serve hot.

RED BEANS AND RICE

SERVES 2+

A little taste of Louisiana, this rice dish stands alone as a meatless meal, or makes a great side dish. A dash of hot sauce may be desired.

$1/4$ cup chopped onion
1 clove garlic, minced, or $1/2$ teaspoon bottled minced garlic
1 cup chicken broth
1 ($14^1/2$-ounce) can crushed tomatoes
$1/2$ teaspoon ground cumin
Salt
Freshly ground black pepper
$1/3$ cup uncooked converted rice
1 (15-ounce) can red kidney beans, rinsed and drained
Chopped fresh cilantro or parsley, optional

1. Coat the inside of a $3^1/2$-quart slow cooker with cooking spray, if desired.

2. Add onion, garlic, broth, crushed tomatoes, and cumin to slow cooker. Season to taste with salt and pepper. Stir well to mix. Add rice and beans and stir again.

3. Cover and cook on High for 3 hours.

4. Serve hot with optional cilantro or parsley for garnish.

MUSHROOM RISOTTO

SERVES 4

This tasty risotto is made with Arborio rice, a short-grain, creamy rice. Cooked in the traditional manner, risotto must be stirred continuously. This rice takes about 2 to 2$\frac{1}{2}$ hours to cook, but only needs to be stirred twice while cooking.

2 tablespoons cold butter, finely diced
2 tablespoons olive oil
2 cups Arborio rice
$\frac{1}{2}$ ounce dried mushrooms, reconstituted in water and drained, or 4 ounces fresh mushrooms, chopped
$\frac{1}{2}$ small onion, chopped
4 cups chicken broth
$\frac{1}{2}$ cup white wine
$\frac{1}{2}$ cup grated or shredded Parmesan cheese

1. Coat the inside of a 3$\frac{1}{2}$-quart slow cooker with cooking spray, if desired.

2. Melt butter and olive oil on High in slow cooker.

3. When butter is melted, stir in rice to coat in the butter/oil mixture. Add mushrooms and onion. Stir in broth.

4. Cover and cook on High for 1 hour. Stir. Re-cover and cook 1 additional hour. Add wine; stir well to mix. Re-cover and cook an additional 15 to 20 minutes. Stir in Parmesan cheese and serve.

RICE PILAF
SERVES 2+

You'll want to have extra rice on hand, even some in the freezer, so feel free to double this recipe. The converted rice cooks perfectly in the slow cooker.

1 small onion, chopped
$1/2$ cup uncooked converted rice
$3/4$ cup chicken broth
$3/4$ cup water
Salt

1. Coat the inside of a $3^1/2$-quart slow cooker with cooking spray, if desired.

2. Add onion, rice, broth, water, and salt to taste.

3. Cover and cook on High for $1^1/2$ hours. Check rice for doneness, and if the rice is still a little bit hard in the center, cook an additional 30 minutes.

WILD RICE WITH PECANS

SERVES 2

Perfect for a holiday table, or an accompaniment to any poultry meal, this rice is a crunchy, satisfying side dish.

1 (4-ounce) package plain wild rice
1 teaspoon salt
1 medium carrot, chopped
1 small onion, chopped
$1/4$ cup dried cranberries
2 cups hot water
$1/2$ cup chopped pecans

1. Coat the inside of a $3^1/2$-quart slow cooker with cooking spray, if desired.

2. Add rice, salt, carrot, onion, and cranberries. Stir in hot water.

3. Cover and cook on High for 3 hours. Turn off slow cooker, uncover, and let rice sit 20 to 30 minutes to allow excess moisture to evaporate.

4. Stir pecans into rice and serve.

BULGUR PILAF

SERVES 2

This side dish can be varied in numerous ways. For a vegetarian main course, use vegetable broth and add in cooked lentils or diced tofu. Spice it up with cumin, red pepper flakes, or diced green chile peppers.

1/2 cup bulgur wheat
1/2 cup fresh mushrooms, chopped
1 small zucchini, chopped
1 clove garlic, minced, or 1/2 teaspoon
   bottled minced garlic
1 1/2 cups chicken broth
1 tablespoon olive oil
3 sprigs fresh thyme, or 1/2 teaspoon
   dried thyme
Salt
Freshly ground black pepper

1. Coat the inside of a 3 1/2-quart slow cooker with cooking spray, if desired.

2. Add all ingredients to the slow cooker and season to taste with salt and pepper. Stir well to mix.

3. Cover and cook on Low for 4 hours. Fluff with a fork, taste, and season again with salt and pepper. Serve hot.

BULGUR, BARLEY, AND WILD RICE MEDLEY

SERVES 2+

A variety of grains cook well in the slow cooker. Combined, they make for a novel side dish. Add a vegetarian protein, such as tofu, to make a one-pot meal. Season to taste when assembling the dish, and then again once cooked.

¼ cup bulgur wheat
¼ cup pearl barley
¼ cup wild rice
2 tablespoons chopped fresh or freeze-dried parsley
2 tablespoons olive oil
1 teaspoon grated lemon rind, no white attached
3 green onions, thinly sliced, including some green parts
1 clove garlic, minced, or ½ teaspoon bottled minced garlic
2 cups chicken broth
Salt
Freshly ground black pepper

1. Coat the inside of a 3½-quart slow cooker with cooking spray, if desired.

2. Add all ingredients to the slow cooker and season to taste with salt and pepper. Stir well to mix.

3. Cover and cook on Low for 4 hours. Fluff with a fork and leave uncovered for 30 minutes, still on Low, to allow excess moisture to evaporate.

4. Fluff again, taste, and season again with salt and pepper. Serve hot.

FENNEL AND TOMATOES
SERVES 2+

Serve this dish warm as a side for meat or fish. For a meal, add two thin tilapia fillets on top of the cooked fennel. Cover and cook until fish is flaky and cooked through, about 30 minutes.

1 medium fennel bulb, trimmed of stalks, cored, and sliced thinly, fronds reserved
1 clove garlic, minced, or $1/2$ teaspoon bottled minced garlic
1 tablespoon balsamic or other favorite vinegar
1 tablespoon olive oil
Salt
Freshly ground black pepper
$11/2$ cups chopped fresh tomatoes, or 1 ($141/2$-ounce) can diced tomatoes, drained

1. Coat the inside of a $31/2$-quart slow cooker with cooking spray or insert a disposable liner, both optional.

2. Add fennel, garlic, vinegar, and olive oil, stirring well to mix. Season to taste with salt and freshly ground black pepper. Stir in tomatoes.

3. Cover and cook on Low for 3 hours.

4. Taste, and season again with salt and pepper. Chop up to 1 tablespoon reserved fronds and sprinkle on top, if desired. Serve hot.

RATATOUILLE

SERVES 2

Ratatouille is great as a side dish or as a topping for meats and fish. Add in a vegetarian protein, such as tofu, and you have a one-pot meal. Chopping the vegetables "roughly" means to chop them into larger chunks, rather than a typical chop. The vegetables will hold their shape a little better in the slow cooker if left a bit larger.

1 small eggplant, roughly chopped
1 small zucchini, roughly chopped
2 cloves garlic, minced, or 1 teaspoon
    bottled minced garlic
1/4 cup chopped onion
1 red bell pepper, cored, seeded, and
    chopped
1 cup chopped fresh tomatoes
1/2 cup sliced fresh mushrooms
1 tablespoon balsamic vinegar
1 tablespoon olive oil
3 sprigs fresh thyme, or 1/2 teaspoon
    dried thyme
Salt
Freshly ground black pepper

1. Coat the inside of a 3 1/2-quart slow cooker with cooking spray or insert a disposable liner, both optional.

2. Add the eggplant, zucchini, garlic, onion, bell pepper, tomatoes, mushrooms, vinegar, and oil. Stir well to mix. Top with fresh thyme sprigs, or stir in dried thyme.

3. Cover and cook on Low for 3 1/2 hours. Stir ratatouille and season to taste with salt and pepper. If vegetables are not done to your liking, cover and continue to cook up to 1 additional hour.

4. Taste, and season again with salt and pepper. Serve hot or at room temperature.

EGGPLANT PARMESAN
SERVES 2

The slow cooker yields eggplant with just the perfect tenderness. Mozzarella cheese may be substituted for the Parmesan, if desired.

1 (8-ounce) can tomato sauce, divided
1 large eggplant, cut into 6 slices
1 teaspoon dried Italian seasoning, divided
$\frac{1}{4}$ cup grated or shredded Parmesan cheese, divided
$\frac{1}{2}$ (15-ounce) carton ricotta cheese, divided

1. Coat the inside of a $3\frac{1}{2}$-quart slow cooker with cooking spray, if desired.

2. Coat the bottom of the slow cooker with about $\frac{1}{2}$ cup of the tomato sauce.

3. Make two stacks, nestled against each other, in the bottom of the slow cooker by beginning with the two largest pieces of eggplant. Sprinkle each with a little Italian seasoning and Parmesan cheese, cover with a little ricotta cheese, and top each with another piece of eggplant and repeat. Pour remaining sauce on top of both stacks of eggplant.

4. Cover and cook on Low for 6 to 7 hours.

5. Remove the stacks to separate serving dishes and spoon any sauce remaining in the slow cooker over the top. Sprinkle with additional Parmesan cheese, if desired.

SPINACH LASAGNA

SERVES 2+

No need to precook the noodles, as the moisture from the sauce and steam created in the slow cooker will cook them perfectly.

1 (10-ounce) package frozen spinach, thawed and squeezed dry
$1/2$ (15-ounce) container ricotta cheese
1 clove garlic, minced, or $1/2$ teaspoon bottled minced garlic
1 teaspoon Italian seasoning, or more to taste
Salt
Freshly ground black pepper
1 ($14^{1/2}$-ounce) can crushed tomatoes
4 uncooked lasagna noodles, broken to fit
1 cup grated mozzarella cheese

1. Coat the inside of a $3^{1/2}$-quart slow cooker with cooking spray, if desired.

2. Mix together the spinach, ricotta cheese, garlic, and Italian seasoning in a small bowl. Season to taste with salt and pepper.

3. Coat the bottom of the slow cooker with about $1/2$ cup crushed tomatoes.

4. Add $1^{1/2}$ noodles on top of the puree in a single layer, breaking if needed to fit. Spread with half of the spinach-ricotta mixture. Top with a little of the tomatoes and sprinkle with half of the mozzarella cheese. Repeat with another identical layer. Finish with a final layer of noodles and remaining sauce. Top with the remaining mozzarella cheese.

5. Cover and cook on Low for $3^{1/2}$ hours. Check to be sure noodles are soft, and serve warm.

DESSERTS

VANILLA CUSTARD

SERVES 2

A little vanilla valentine for two, this custard can be made in the morning and refrigerated until serving after dinner.

Softened butter, for ramekins
1 large egg
2 tablespoons granulated sugar
$1/3$ cup milk
$1/3$ heavy whipping cream
$1/2$ teaspoon vanilla extract
$1/4$ teaspoon ground nutmeg

1. Butter the insides of two $1/2$-cup ramekins. Place two cookie cutters, Mason jar rings, or rings made from aluminum foil (see page 13) inside the slow cooker.

2. Whisk together the egg, sugar, milk, cream, and vanilla, mixing well. Divide mixture evenly between the two ramekins and cover with plastic wrap. Place each ramekin on a cutter or ring. Add hot water to the slow cooker to come halfway up the sides of the ramekins.

3. Cover and cook on Low for 2 hours. Custard will still be slightly loose. Remove ramekins carefully to avoid getting burned. Cool for 30 minutes, then refrigerate to serve cold.

LEMON CAKE

SERVES 2

Light and airy, this lemon cake is fit for two.

¼ cup butter, room temperature
¼ cup granulated sugar
1 large egg
½ cup self-rising flour
¼ teaspoon baking soda
Grated rind of ½ lemon, no white attached
2 teaspoons milk

FOR DRIZZLE:
½ cup confectioners' sugar
1–2 teaspoons lemon juice

* To make your own self-rising flour, mix 1
  cup all-purpose flour with ½ to 1 teaspoon
  salt and 1½ teaspoons baking powder.

1. Butter and flour the inside of a 5-inch round cake pan. Line bottom with wax paper. Butter and flour the paper.

2. Place a cookie cutter, Mason jar ring, or a ring made from aluminum foil (see page 13) inside the slow cooker. Add hot water to a 1-inch depth and turn slow cooker to the High heat setting.

3. Whisk together the butter, sugar, and egg. Add the flour, baking soda, lemon rind, and milk, and whisk well to mix. Pour the mixture into the prepared pan, and cover tightly with foil. Transfer the pan to the slow cooker, placing it on top of the ring. Add additional hot water to come halfway up the sides of the pan.

4. Cover, change the heat setting to Low, and cook for 1½ hours, until a toothpick inserted in the center comes out clean. If not fully cooked, replace cover and cook up to an additional 30 minutes. Remove pan carefully to avoid getting burned. Cool briefly, then run a knife around the inside of the pan to loosen the cake. Invert the cake onto a serving plate, and remove the wax paper.

5. Prepare the drizzle by stirring the lemon juice into the sugar. Pour over warm cake and serve warm or cooled to room temperature.

LEMON CREAMS
SERVES 2

When Meyer lemon season arrives, I'm ready for dessert. These lemon creams take full advantage of the Meyer lemon's superior tart-sweet flavor. Although they are tempting when warm, do wait for the creams to chill before eating.

¼ cup granulated sugar
2 tablespoons Meyer lemon juice
¼ teaspoon grated Meyer lemon zest rind, no white attached
2 large egg yolks
½ cup heavy cream

1. Butter the insides of two ½-cup ramekins. Place two cookie cutters, Mason jar rings, or rings made from aluminum foil (see page 13) inside the slow cooker. Add hot water to a 1-inch depth and turn slow cooker on to the Low heat setting.

2. Stir together the sugar, lemon juice, and lemon rind in a small bowl. Whisk together the egg yolks and cream in another small bowl. Pour the lemon juice mixture into the cream mixture and whisk well to mix. Divide mixture evenly between the two ramekins and cover with plastic wrap. Place each ramekin on a cutter or ring. Add additional hot water to come halfway up the sides of the ramekins.

3. Cover and cook on Low for 2 hours. The mixture will still be slightly loose. Remove ramekins carefully to avoid getting burned. Cool for 30 minutes, then refrigerate to serve cold.

LEMON CURD
MAKES 2½ CUPS

Lemon curd is a versatile refrigerator staple used in tarts, to spread between cake layers, or to slather on an English muffin. Mixing equal portions of lemon curd with whipped cream makes a lovely mousse-like topping for berries or filling for meringue cookies. Making the lemon curd in a slow cooker frees the cook from tedious stirring at the stove. Select your bowl before starting the recipe. A microplane grater makes zesting easy.

3 whole lemons
1 cup granulated sugar
7 tablespoons unsalted butter, cut into
   ½-inch dice, room temperature
2 large eggs
2 large egg yolks

1. Select a 4-cup bowl that fits into the slow cooker and set aside. (A straight-sided glass bowl is ideal). Place a cookie cutter, Mason jar ring, or a ring made from aluminum foil (see page 13) inside the slow cooker. Prepare an aluminum foil sling (see page 13) and place on top of cutter or ring. Add hot water to a 2-inch depth and turn slow cooker to the High heat setting and cover.

2. Zest all three lemons, being careful not to zest the bitter white pith, and add zest to the bowl. Juice the lemons over a strainer into the bowl and discard contents of the strainer.

3. Stir in sugar and add butter cubes. Move the bowl to the slow cooker, on top of the sling. Cover and cook on High until butter melts, about 20 minutes, stirring occasionally. Carefully remove bowl when butter is melted.

4. Beat eggs and egg yolks together in a separate bowl until combined. Strain the eggs through a mesh strainer into the butter-lemon juice mixture and stir well.

5. Move the bowl with the lemon mixture to the slow cooker and place on top of the sling (with ring underneath) so the bowl is not touching the bottom of the slow cooker. Cover the top of the bowl tightly with a piece of aluminum foil. Add enough hot tap water to the slow cooker to come halfway up the sides of the bowl.

6. Cover and cook on Low for 2 hours, stirring thoroughly twice during cooking. The curd is ready when it reaches 170 degrees on an instant-read thermometer. Carefully remove the bowl from the slow cooker using the four pieces of aluminum foil to cradle the bowl. Curd will thicken as it cools. Transfer to a clean storage container. Lemon curd freezes beautifully (it doesn't freeze solid and can be spooned out easily) or can be stored in the refrigerator for up to two weeks.

CHOCOLATE FONDUE

SERVES 2+

Fondue is an easy, no-fuss dessert—and it's fun! Use cut-up fruit, whole strawberries, chunks of pound cake, or long pretzel rods for dipping. Punch up the flavor with a tablespoon of liqueur such as Grand Marnier or Kahlúa.

1 cup semisweet chocolate chips
3/4 cup heavy whipping cream
2 teaspoons light corn syrup
1/4 teaspoon salt

1. Coat the inside of a $3^{1}/_{2}$-quart slow cooker with cooking spray, if desired.

2. Stir together all the ingredients in the slow cooker.

3. Cover and cook on Low for 1 hour. Whisk the mixture briefly to smooth.

4. Serve with a variety of dippers.

CHOCOLATE CAKE
SERVES 2+

This sticky batter turns into a lovely, moist cake. The chocolate drizzle is optional, but delightful.

1/3 cup semisweet chocolate chips
4 teaspoons milk
5 tablespoons butter, room temperature
1/3 cup light or dark brown sugar
2 teaspoons honey
1 large egg, plus 1 egg yolk
1 cup self-rising flour*
1 1/2 teaspoons unsweetened cocoa powder
1/4 teaspoon baking powder

FOR DRIZZLE:
1/2 cup confectioners' sugar
1–2 teaspoons unsweetened cocoa powder
1 or more teaspoons milk or water

* To make your own self-rising flour, mix 1 cup all-purpose flour with 1/2 to 1 teaspoon salt and 1 1/2 teaspoons baking powder.

1. Butter the inside of a 5-inch baking pan. Line bottom with wax paper. Butter the paper.

2. Place a cookie cutter, Mason jar ring, or a ring made from aluminum foil (see page 13) inside the slow cooker. Add hot water to a 1-inch depth and turn slow cooker on to the High heat setting.

3. Stir the chocolate chips and milk in a small glass custard cup. Place on top of ring in slow cooker to melt while preparing cake.

4. Using a hand mixer, beat together butter and sugar in a medium bowl. Whisk in the egg and yolk. Remove custard cup from slow cooker and scrape chocolate into butter mixture. Fold in the flour, cocoa powder, and baking powder until incorporated. Scrape the mixture into the prepared pan, and smooth out the top with a spatula coated with cooking spray (batter is sticky) and cover tightly with foil. Transfer the pan to the slow cooker, placing it on top of the ring. Add additional hot water to come halfway up the sides of the pan.

5. Cover, and cook on High for 1 1/2 hours. The center will have fallen and may be slightly moist. Remove pan carefully to avoid getting burned. Cool briefly, then run a knife around the inside of the pan to loosen the cake. Invert the cake onto a serving plate, and remove the wax paper.

6. Prepare the drizzle by combining the confectioners' sugar, cocoa powder, and milk or water until it reaches a pourable consistency. Drizzle over warm cake. Serve warm, or cool cake to room temperature and serve.

BANANA BREAD

We love banana bread, but not for days on end. This small loaf is perfect for a treat lasting a day or two. The paper towels prevent the natural build-up of steam from potentially dripping on the loaf and making the bread soggy.

1/2 cup, plus 2 tablespoons all-purpose flour
1/4 teaspoon baking soda
Pinch of salt
3 tablespoons vegetable oil
1/4 cup light or dark brown sugar
1 large egg yolk
1/2 cup mashed banana
1 tablespoon milk
1/2 teaspoon vanilla extract
1/4 cup walnuts, chopped

1. Place a cookie cutter, Mason jar ring, or a ring made from aluminum foil (see page 13) inside the slow cooker. Butter a 5-inch mini loaf pan and set aside.

2. Whisk together the flour, baking soda, and salt in a small bowl. Add oil, brown sugar, egg yolk, banana, milk, and vanilla, stirring just until flour mixture is incorporated. Fold in nuts.

3. Scrape batter into prepared loaf pan. Transfer loaf pan to sit on top of ring in slow cooker.

4. Place paper towels, still attached together, folded as necessary, over the top of the slow cooker. Cover and cook on High for 2 hours. When a toothpick inserted in the middle of the loaf comes out clean, the bread is cooked. If it does not emerge clean, continue cooking an additional 30 minutes.

5. Carefully remove the loaf pan from the slow cooker. Run a knife around the inside of the loaf pan and turn the loaf out onto a rack to cool. Serve warm or at room temperature.

APPLE CRISP
SERVES 2+

All the goodness of an apple pie with none of the fuss! Select your favorite cooking apple for this recipe. Let your conscience be your guide, but vanilla ice cream seems to be in order here.

2 apples, peeled, cored, and chopped
3 tablespoons granulated sugar
1 teaspoon cornstarch
1/4 teaspoon ground ginger
1/4 teaspoon ground cinnamon
1 tablespoon lemon juice

TOPPING:
1/3 cup all-purpose flour
2 tablespoons light or dark brown sugar
2 tablespoons granulated sugar
1/4 teaspoon ground cinnamon
Pinch of ground nutmeg
2 tablespoons cold butter, cut into small dice
1/2 cup chopped walnuts or pecans

1. Coat the inside of a 3 1/2-quart slow cooker with cooking spray, if desired.

2. Add the apples to the slow cooker. Stir together the sugar, cornstarch, ginger, and cinnamon in a small bowl and sprinkle over apples. Drizzle lemon juice over apples and stir.

3. For the topping, stir together the flour, sugars, cinnamon, and nutmeg in a small bowl. Using fingers or two forks, work the butter into the flour mixture until crumbly. Sprinkle topping and nuts over apples.

4. Cover and cook on High for 2 hours. Test to be sure apples are adequately softened. Uncover and continue to cook up to 30 minutes to crisp the topping. Serve warm.

POACHED PEARS

Poached pears are an elegant end to a meal. Plus, a fruit dessert always makes me feel virtuous. Serve on top of ice cream if you are feeling wicked.

1/4 cup granulated sugar
3/4 cup red wine
Strip of orange peel, no white attached
1/2 small cinnamon stick, or 1/4 teaspoon
   ground cinnamon
2 whole cloves
2 pears, peeled, quartered, and cored

1. Coat the inside of a 3 1/2-quart slow cooker with cooking spray, if desired.

2. Turn the slow cooker to High and add the sugar, wine, orange peel, cinnamon, and cloves. Stir well to mix. Cook for 1 hour.

3. Add pears and cook 2 hours. Remove to a bowl to cool slightly before serving.

GRANOLA

MAKES 4 CUPS

For breakfast, snacks, or as a topping for fruit or ice cream, customize this recipe by creating your own fruit and nut mixtures. This granola produces oats that only slightly cling together. For a crunchier, cluster-type of granola, increase the honey by up to 1 cup. Experiment until you find the consistency you prefer. If adding more honey, watch carefully during the last 30 minutes of cooking time, as the honey can cause excess browning.

$\frac{1}{4}$ cup butter, room temperature

4 cups rolled oats

$\frac{1}{2}$ cup chopped mixed nuts, such as almonds, walnuts, and pecans

$\frac{1}{2}$ cup unsweetened shredded coconut, optional

$\frac{1}{2}$ cup chopped dried fruit, such as dates, raisins, apricots, cranberries

$\frac{1}{4}$ cup honey

1. Coat the inside of a $3\frac{1}{2}$-quart slow cooker with cooking spray, if desired.

2. Melt butter on High in the slow cooker, about 20 to 30 minutes.

3. Stir in oats, coating with the butter. Add nuts, coconut, if using, and dried fruit. Stir well to mix. Pour in honey and stir again.

4. Cover the crock with two layers of paper towels, and then the lid. Cook 3 hours on High, stirring once or twice during cooking time. Granola can cook up to 4 hours; watch carefully to prevent excessive browning.

5. Spread on a cookie sheet to cool. Store in airtight containers at room temperature, refrigerated, or in the freezer for up to 3 months.

DIPS AND APPETIZERS

HOT CHEESE DIP

MAKES ABOUT 2 CUPS

It's convenient to purchase pre-cooked bacon. Scissors make easy work of cutting it into strips.

1 (8-ounce) package cream cheese, softened and cut into small chunks
2 cups shredded sharp Cheddar cheese, or other favorite cheese
1/2 cup half-and-half
1 teaspoon Worcestershire sauce
1/2 teaspoon dried minced onion
1/2 teaspoon Dijon mustard
4 pieces cooked bacon, cut into small strips

1. Coat the inside of a $3^{1}/_{2}$-quart slow cooker with cooking spray, if desired.

2. Add all ingredients except bacon. Stir well to mix.

3. Cover and cook on Low for $1^{1}/_{2}$ hours. Stir in bacon before serving.

4. Serve with crusty bread or crackers.

KALE AND ARTICHOKE DIP
MAKES ABOUT 2 CUPS

Traditionally made with spinach, this dip is even heartier made with kale. Bags of pre-washed, chopped fresh kale are often available in the produce section. Chop the kale further into bite-sized pieces.

1 (6-ounce) jar marinated artichoke hearts, drained well, and chopped
1 cup mayonnaise
1/2 (8-ounce) package cream cheese, cut into small chunks
3/4 cup grated Parmesan cheese
1 clove garlic, minced, or 1/2 teaspoon bottled minced garlic
2 cups chopped fresh kale

1. Coat the inside of a 3 1/2-quart slow cooker with cooking spray, if desired.

2. Add all ingredients to slow cooker. Stir well to mix.

3. Cover and cook on Low for 1 1/2 hours. Stir halfway through cooking time. Turn heat setting to Warm, if available, and serve from slow cooker.

4. Serve with crusty bread or crackers.

SPICY MIXED NUTS

MAKES 4 CUPS

These nuts make a handy hostess or holiday gift. The mix freezes well for longer term storage; otherwise it stays fresh for about 2 weeks. The last hour of cooking uncovered helps to evaporate any excess moisture.

1/4 cup butter, room temperature
1 1/3 cups pecan halves
1 1/3 cups walnut halves
1 1/3 cups whole almonds
1 teaspoon salt
1 teaspoon dried oregano
1 teaspoon dried basil
1 teaspoon dried thyme
1/4 teaspoon garlic powder
1/4 teaspoon onion powder
1/4 teaspoon cayenne pepper, optional

1. Coat the inside of a 3 1/2-quart slow cooker with cooking spray, if desired.

2. Add butter to slow cooker, cover, and cook on High for 20 minutes, until butter is melted.

3. Stir remaining ingredients into the butter, add nuts, and stir until nuts are thoroughly coated with the herbs and seasonings.

4. Cover the top of the slow cooker with a layer of paper towels. Cover and cook on Low for 2 hours. Uncover and continue to cook 1 more hour. Transfer the nuts to a large baking sheet to cool before storing in airtight containers.

CRAB DIP

Warm and creamy, this dip will take you right back to summer at the beach.

½ (8-ounce) package cream cheese, cut into
    small chunks
½ cup mayonnaise
3 tablespoons grated Parmesan cheese
3 tablespoons chopped fresh or freeze-dried
    chives
1 teaspoon Worcestershire sauce
1 (6-ounce) can crabmeat, drained, or ½ cup
    fresh crabmeat, picked over
Snipped fresh chives, optional

1. Coat the inside of a $3^1/_2$-quart slow cooker with cooking spray, if desired.

2. Add all ingredients to slow cooker. Stir well to mix.

3. Cover and cook on Low for $1^1/_2$ hours. Stir well. Top with chives, if desired.

4. Serve with crackers or pita chips.

WHITE BEAN SPREAD

MAKES ABOUT 1 1/2 CUPS

Thick and hearty, this dip is backed with protein and really satisfies.

1 (15-ounce) can cannellini beans, rinsed and
   drained
1/2 cup chicken broth
1 tablespoon olive oil, plus more for drizzling
2 cloves garlic, minced, or 1/2 teaspoon
   bottled minced garlic
1 sprig fresh rosemary, or a pinch of dried
   rosemary
Salt
Freshly ground black pepper

1. Coat the inside of a 3 1/2-quart slow cooker with cooking spray, if desired.

2. Add all ingredients to slow cooker, and stir well to mix.

3. Cover and cook on Low for 3 hours. Remove rosemary sprig and mash beans by hand, using a potato masher. Transfer dip to a serving bowl and drizzle with additional olive oil.

4. Serve warm with pita chips or crackers.

BLACK BEAN DIP

MAKES ABOUT 2 CUPS

Serve this rustic and flavorful dip with the bowl-shaped corn or tortilla chips. When chopping the pepper, be careful to remove the interior membrane and all the seeds. Wash hands thoroughly after chopping.

1 (15-ounce) can black beans, rinsed and drained

$1/2$ jalapeño pepper, finely chopped

1 small onion, finely chopped

$1/2$ cup favorite jarred salsa

$1/4$ cup sour cream

1 cup shredded cheese (Cheddar, Mexican blend, or other favorite)

1. Coat the inside of a $3^1/2$-quart slow cooker with cooking spray, if desired.

2. Add the beans, pepper, onion, and salsa to slow cooker. Stir well to mix.

3. Cover and cook on Low for 2 hours. Stir in sour cream and cheese, and then change the heat setting to warm.

4. Serve from the slow cooker with corn chips or tortilla chips.

BASICS

CHICKEN STOCK
MAKES 4 CUPS

Homemade chicken stock is so tasty—and the cook can control the ingredients, especially the sodium level. Store in small quantities for maximum flexibility.

2 pounds chicken wings, or a combination of wings and bones
1 medium carrot, chopped
1 small onion, chopped
1 rib celery, chopped
6 black peppercorns
1 bay leaf, optional
Salt, optional

1. Coat the inside of a 3^1/$_2$-quart slow cooker with cooking spray or insert a disposable liner, both optional.

2. Transfer all ingredients to slow cooker. Cover with 4 cups water.

3. Cover and cook on High for 2 hours. Skim off any foam that has formed on the top. Replace cover, reduce temperature to Low, and cook 3 to 4 more hours.

4. Strain contents of slow cooker over a large bowl, and allow liquid to cool to room temperature. Store in plastic containers or resealable plastic bags. Refrigerate for up to a week, or freeze for up to 3 months.

BEEF STOCK

MAKES 4 CUPS

Handy for soup bases, beef stock is heartier in flavor than chicken stock.

1½ pounds beef bones
1 medium carrot, roughly chopped
1 small onion, roughly chopped
1 rib celery, roughly chopped
6 black peppercorns
1 teaspoon dried thyme
Salt, optional

1. Coat the inside of a 3½-quart slow cooker with cooking spray or insert a disposable liner, both optional.

2. Transfer all ingredients to slow cooker. Cover with 4 cups water.

3. Cover and cook on High for 2 hours. Skim off any foam that has formed on the top. Replace cover, reduce the temperature to Low, and cook 3 to 4 more hours.

4. Strain contents of slow cooker over a large bowl, and allow liquid to cool to room temperature. Store in plastic containers or resealable plastic bags. Refrigerate for up to a week, or freeze for up to 3 months.

ROASTED GARLIC HEADS

MAKES 3 HEADS

Roasted garlic slathered on toasted French bread is a treat. The garlic turns nutty and smooth and has a tad of sweetness to it. Keep it on hand for stirring into soups, stews, or mashed potatoes. Try some in a vinaigrette dressing for salad.

3 heads garlic
2 tablespoons olive oil, divided
Salt

1. Coat the inside of a $3^1/_2$-quart slow cooker with cooking spray, if desired.

2. Slice off the top from each head of garlic, removing the top $^1/_2$ inch and exposing the cloves. Transfer the heads to the slow cooker and drizzle each with olive oil. Sprinkle with salt.

3. Cover and cook on Low 4 to 5 hours. Remove to a plate and allow to cool. Squeeze the softened cloves out of the head and into a storage container. Cooked garlic will keep about a week in the refrigerator.

CARAMELIZED ONIONS

MAKES 2 CUPS

Slow-cooked onions are a savory condiment for topping everything from sandwiches to toast. For a twist, add chopped cooked bacon during the last hour of cooking.

2–2½ pounds sweet onions, such as Vidalia, Walla Walla, or Texas Sweets, sliced
2–3 tablespoons olive oil
3 tablespoons port wine

1. Coat the inside of a 3½-quart slow cooker with cooking spray, if desired.

2. Transfer onions to the slow cooker and drizzle with olive oil. Stir well to mix.

3. Cover and cook on Low 9 hours, stirring once or twice during cooking time, if possible.

4. Stir in port wine and turn slow cooker to High. Leave uncovered and cook 1 hour to allow excess moisture to evaporate.

5. Remove to a bowl and allow to cool. Transfer to airtight containers and keep refrigerated for up to 2 weeks.

MARINARA SAUCE

While I'll always have jarred sauce in my pantry, sometimes I like to control the spices myself. This is my go-to recipe for homemade sauce.

1 (14$\frac{1}{2}$-ounce) can crushed tomatoes
1 (14$\frac{1}{2}$-ounce) can diced tomatoes
$\frac{1}{2}$ (6-ounce) can tomato paste
1 small onion, chopped
2 cloves garlic, minced, or 1 teaspoon bottled minced garlic
1 bay leaf
2 tablespoons chopped fresh basil, or 2 teaspoons dried basil
1 teaspoon dried oregano
2 teaspoons light or dark brown sugar
2 teaspoons balsamic vinegar, or other favorite vinegar
Salt
Freshly ground black pepper

1. Coat the inside of a 3$\frac{1}{2}$-quart slow cooker with cooking spray or insert a disposable liner, both optional.

2. Add all ingredients to slow cooker, except salt and pepper. Stir well to mix.

3. Cover and cook on Low 7 to 8 hours. Season to taste with salt and pepper.

4. Remove and discard bay leaf. Cool sauce and store in an airtight container in the refrigerator for up to 5 days, or freeze for up to 3 months.

GINGER PEACH BUTTER

MAKES ABOUT 2 CUPS

Perfect on a tender biscuit, toasted English muffin, or dolloped on a scoop of vanilla ice cream, this peach butter is a handy refrigerator jam to have on hand. The fresh ginger makes all the difference in this recipe.

1 (16-ounce) package frozen peaches, thawed and chopped, or 1 pound fresh peaches, peeled and chopped
$1/2$ cup granulated sugar
1 teaspoon lemon juice
$1/4$ teaspoon ground cinnamon
$1/2$ teaspoon freshly grated ginger, or $1/4$ teaspoon ground ginger
1 teaspoon quick-cooking Tapioca

1. Coat the inside of a $3^1/2$-quart slow cooker with cooking spray or insert a disposable liner, both optional.

2. Add the peaches, sugar, lemon juice, cinnamon, and ginger to slow cooker. Stir well to mix.

3. Cover and cook on Low for 2 hours. Change the heat setting to High and stir in tapioca. Cover and cook an additional 30 to 60 minutes to thicken. Cool to near room temperature, and store in airtight containers in the refrigerator for up to 2 weeks, or freeze for up to 3 months.

CINNAMON-GINGER APPLESAUCE

MAKES 2 CUPS

Applesauce with no additives and no stirring for the cook! Use your favorite apple—I like Jonathan, McIntosh, or Golden Delicious for this recipe. Adjust the liquid and sugar to your taste.

1½ **pounds apples (about 3 large), peeled, cored, and cut into chunks**
½ **cup cranberry or apple juice**
1 **tablespoon granulated sugar**

1. Coat the inside of a 3½-quart slow cooker with cooking spray, if desired.

2. Add all ingredients to slow cooker. Stir well to mix.

3. Cover and cook on Low for 4 hours. Mash apples by hand using a potato masher. Cool to near room temperature, and store in airtight containers in the refrigerator for up to 2 weeks, or freeze for up to 3 months. Serve warm, at room temperature, or chilled.

CRANBERRY SAUCE
MAKES 1 1/2 CUPS

When bags of fresh cranberries are on sale, I snag a couple of bags for the freezer. Then I can make fresh cranberry sauce anytime.

1 (12-ounce) bag fresh cranberries, thawed if frozen
1 cup granulated sugar
2 tablespoons Grand Marnier, or other flavored liqueur, optional

1. Coat the inside of a 3 1/2-quart slow cooker with cooking spray, if desired.

2. Add all ingredients to slow cooker. Stir well to mix.

3. Cover and cook on Low for 4 hours. Stir and taste for sweetness, adding more sugar if desired. Cool to near room temperature, and store in airtight containers in the refrigerator for up to a week. Serve chilled or at room temperature.

INDEX

METRIC CONVERSION CHART

VOLUME MEASUREMENTS		WEIGHT MEASUREMENTS		TEMPERATURE CONVERSION	
U.S.	Metric	U.S.	Metric	Fahrenheit	Celsius
1 teaspoon	5 ml	1/2 ounce	15 g	250	120
1 tablespoon	15 ml	1 ounce	30 g	300	150
1/4 cup	60 ml	3 ounces	90 g	325	160
1/3 cup	75 ml	4 ounces	115 g	350	180
1/2 cup	125 ml	8 ounces	225 g	375	190
2/3 cup	150 ml	12 ounces	350 g	400	200
3/4 cup	175 ml	1 pound	450 g	425	220
1 cup	250 ml	2 1/4 pounds	1 kg	450	230

ABOUT THE AUTHOR

James Beard Award winner Cynthia Graubart is passionate about bringing families together at the table. Now, along with her husband, she is an empty nester. Co-author of three books, she is also a culinary television producer and cooking teacher. Her previous books include co-authoring *Mastering the Art of Southern Cooking* (2013 James Beard Award) and *Southern Biscuits*, both with Nathalie Dupree. Her first book was *The One-Armed Cook: Quick and Easy Recipes, Smart Meal Plans, and Savvy Advice for New (and not-so-new) Moms*. She is a member of the International Association of Culinary Professionals (IACP), Les Dames d'Escoffier (LDEI) and has served on the board of the Atlanta Community Food Bank.

NOTES

NOTES

NOTES